AF705831

# ASIA BOND MONITOR

## MARCH 2026

ASIAN DEVELOPMENT BANK

ADB

6 ADB Avenue, Mandaluyong City, 1550 Metro Manila, Philippines
Tel +63 2 8632 4444; Fax +63 2 8636 2444
www.adb.org



ISBN 978-92-9277-727-2 (print); 978-92-9277-728-9 (PDF); 978-92-9277-729-6 (ebook)
ISSN 2219-1518 (print), 2219-1526 (PDF)
Publication Stock No. SGP260088-2
DOI: http://dx.doi.org/10.22617/SGP260088-2



Note:
ADB recognizes "China" as the People's Republic of China; "Hanoi" as Ha Noi; "Hong Kong" and "Hongkong" as Hong Kong, China; "Korea" and "South Korea" as the Republic of Korea; and "Vietnam" as Viet Nam.

Cover design by Paolo Almazar.

# Contents

## Emerging East Asian Local Currency Bond Markets: A Regional Update

# Emerging East Asian Local Currency Bond Markets: A Regional Update

# Executive Summary

## Recent Trends in Emerging East Asian Financial Markets

Financial markets in emerging East Asia remained resilient between 3 November 2025 and 6 February 2026 amid global market turbulence, supported by sound economic fundamentals and accommodative monetary stances.[1] Episodes of volatility weighed on regional financial markets—particularly in November 2025 over valuation concerns related to artificial intelligence (AI) and in January 2026 over geopolitical and trade tensions. However, better-than-expected economic growth performance in the fourth quarter (Q4) of 2025 and improved sentiment in AI-related sectors bolstered regional financial markets.

During the review period, regional equity markets gained 4.2% (market-weighted average), with net portfolio inflows recorded in most equity markets. As global uncertainties heightened, the United States (US) dollar weakened 2.0% relative to regional currencies (gross-domestic-product-weighted average). Meanwhile, risk premiums, as measured by credit default swap spreads, posted mixed performances over market-specific factors. Local currency (LCY) 10-year government bond yields rose in the region, tracking yields in advanced markets and responding to domestic developments.

Financial markets are expected to remain resilient amid a broadly balanced risk outlook. On the upside, macroeconomic conditions in the region remain stable and accommodative monetary policies provide a buffer against unfavorable shocks. Continued AI investments and advances could sustain corporate earnings, facilitate productivity improvements, and attract additional portfolio and direct investments. Some downside risks remain, including (i) possible prolonged weakness in the People's Republic of China's (PRC) property market; (ii) abrupt changes in investor sentiment, particularly toward AI; (iii) uncertainty in the pace and direction of US monetary policy; and (iv) unexpected trade and geopolitical developments.

## Snapshot of Local Currency Bond Markets in Emerging East Asia

The emerging East Asian LCY bond market expanded 2.1% quarter-on-quarter (q-o-q) in Q4 2025 to reach USD30.6 trillion at the end of December. The bond market's expansion slowed from 3.2% q-o-q in the third quarter (Q3) of 2025, largely due to a decline in issuance, which contracted 11.1% q-o-q in Q4 2025 to USD2.9 trillion on reduced issuance for both government and corporate bonds. The PRC remained the main driver of the region's LCY bond market expansion, accounting for 81.7% of the regional bond stock at the end of December. Association of Southeast Asian Nations (ASEAN) member economies' aggregate bond stock reached USD2.7 trillion, comprising 8.8% of the regional total—but their aggregate issuance in Q4 2025 (USD659.8 billion) contributed 22.8% to the region's total quarterly issuance.

Government bonds outstanding rose 2.0% q-o-q to USD19.9 trillion at the end of Q4 2025, slowing from an expansion of 3.7% q-o-q in Q3 2025. Most regional governments front-loaded their annual issuance in earlier quarters and reduced issuance in Q4 2025. Government bond issuance fell 22.0% q-o-q to USD1.1 trillion in Q4 2025. Corporate bonds outstanding reached USD10.0 trillion, posting a slower expansion of 2.3% q-o-q versus 2.5% q-o-q in Q3 2025 due to reduced issuance in the PRC over economic uncertainty and a large volume of maturities in the Republic of Korea and most ASEAN economies. Emerging East Asia's aggregate corporate bond issuance fell 3.3% q-o-q in Q4 2025 to USD1.1 trillion.

The size-weighted average tenor of Treasury bonds outstanding in emerging East Asia was 9.1 years at the end of December, with Treasury bonds in ASEAN markets having a longer average tenor of 9.4 years. The region's size-weighted average maturity of Treasury bond issuances in Q4 2025 declined to 8.1 years from 11.4 years in Q3 2025 due to increased issuance of short-term

[1] Emerging East Asia is defined to include member states of the Association of Southeast Asian Nations plus the People's Republic of China; Hong Kong, China; and the Republic of Korea.

bonds. Banks remained the largest investor group in the region's LCY Treasury bond market, holding 35.7% of the aggregate stock at the end of 2025, followed by insurance companies and pension funds (29.2%), foreign investors (10.7%), and all other investors (24.4%).

## Snapshot of ASEAN+3 Sustainable Bond Markets

ASEAN+3's sustainable bonds outstanding reached USD1.0 trillion at the end of 2025, accounting for 18.5% of the global total.[2] The market was buoyed by record-high issuance of USD275.9 billion during the year amid accommodative monetary stances in the region. ASEAN+3 led all global regions in sustainable bond issuance in 2025, representing 29.8% of the global total and exceeding the 29.3% share of the European Union 20 (EU-20). ASEAN markets' sustainable bonds outstanding (USD121.4 billion) and issuance (USD32.8 billion) each accounted for 11.9% of the respective ASEAN+3 total in 2025, exceeding their corresponding shares of 5.9% and 3.7% in the general bond market. LCY financing accounted for 73.4% of outstanding bonds and 78.4% of issuance in the ASEAN+3 sustainable bond market, compared with LCY financing's corresponding shares of 90.9% and 87.7% in the EU-20.

The private sector is the major financier in ASEAN+3 sustainable bond markets, accounting for 68.7% of outstanding bonds and 70.2% of issuance in 2025. ASEAN markets had lower average shares of corporate financing (46.6% of outstanding bonds and 47.6% of issuance), due to their relatively smaller LCY corporate bond markets. Short-term financing is prevalent in ASEAN+3's sustainable bond markets due to a relatively high share of private sector financing—with 73.2% of outstanding bonds and 80.2% of issued bonds in 2025 carrying tenors of 5 years or less. In the EU-20, the corresponding shares were 45.1% and 31.4%, respectively. The size-weighted average tenors in ASEAN+3 in 2025 were 4.5 years for bonds outstanding and 5.1 years for issuance, compared to the EU-20's 8.0 years and 8.4 years, respectively.

2 ASEAN+3 comprises the member states of the Association of Southeast Asian Nations (ASEAN) plus the People's Republic of China; Hong Kong, China; Japan; and the Republic of Korea.

# Developments in Regional Financial Conditions

Emerging East Asian financial markets remained resilient amid global headwinds between 3 November 2025 and 6 February 2026, supported by sound economic fundamentals and accommodative monetary stances across the region.[1] There was a brief spike in market volatility in November 2025 on concerns over artificial intelligence (AI) valuations, which eased the following month and intensified again in January 2026 over geopolitical and trade tensions. Better-than-expected economic growth performance in the fourth quarter (Q4) of 2025 in most regional economies and improved sentiment on tech stocks bolstered regional financial markets amid lingering global uncertainty. During the review period, emerging East Asian equity markets gained, supported by net portfolio inflows, and regional currencies appreciated against the United States (US) dollar (**Table A**). Risk premiums diverged over market-specific factors. Regional 10-year government bond yields rose, broadly tracking movements in advanced economies and responding to priced-in domestic conditions.

Market volatility rose amid heightened global uncertainties in January 2026. Following progress on trade agreements between the US and several Asian economies in October 2025, global uncertainty—as measured by trade policy uncertainty and geopolitical risk indicators, and market volatility captured by the Chicago Board Options Exchange Volatility Index (VIX)—eased in November–December 2025. (**Figure A**). The VIX index spiked briefly in the third week of November amid AI-valuation fears and concerns that the Federal Reserve (Fed) might not cut interest rates in December.[2] Volatility ebbed following the Fed's rate cut at its December meeting and as AI concerns eased. January saw renewed volatility amid

**Table A: Changes in Financial Conditions in Major Advanced Economies and Select Emerging East Asian Markets from 3 November 2025 to 6 February 2026**

| | 2-Year Government Bond Yield (bps) | 10-Year Government Bond Yield (bps) | 5-Year Credit Default Swap Spread (bps) | Equity Index (%) | FX Rate (%) |
|---|---|---|---|---|---|
| **Major Advanced Economies** | | | | | |
| Euro Area | 9 | 18 | – | 5.6 | 2.6 |
| Japan | 36 | 56 | 5.9 | 10.3 | (1.9) |
| United States | (11) | 10 | – | 1.2 | – |
| **Select Emerging East Asian Markets** | | | | | |
| People's Republic of China | (5) | 2 | 3.2 | 2.2 | 2.7 |
| Hong Kong, China | (30) | 15 | – | 1.5 | (0.5) |
| Indonesia | 15 | 25 | 4.4 | (4.1) | (1.2) |
| Republic of Korea | 33 | 62 | 0.1 | 20.5 | (2.2) |
| Malaysia | (10) | 7 | (1.1) | 6.8 | 6.4 |
| Philippines | (22) | 2 | 2.8 | 9.7 | 0.4 |
| Singapore | (3) | 12 | – | 11.0 | 2.6 |
| Thailand | (16) | 13 | (1.9) | 3.4 | 2.6 |
| Viet Nam | 29 | 27 | (7.3) | 8.6 | 1.3 |

( ) = negative, – = not available, bps = basis points, FX = foreign exchange.

Note: FX rates are presented against the United States dollar. A positive (negative) value for the FX rate indicates the appreciation (depreciation) of the local currency against the United States dollar.

Source: *AsianBondsOnline* calculations based on Bloomberg LP data.

[1] Emerging East Asia is defined to include member states of the Association of Southeast Asian Nations plus the People's Republic of China; Hong Kong, China; and the Republic of Korea.

[2] Per CME FedWatch, on 19 November, there was a 30.1% probability that the Fed would not cut the federal funds rate at its December meeting.

**Figure A: Trade Policy Uncertainty, Geopolitical Risk, and Chicago Board Options Exchange Volatility—Daily Indexes**

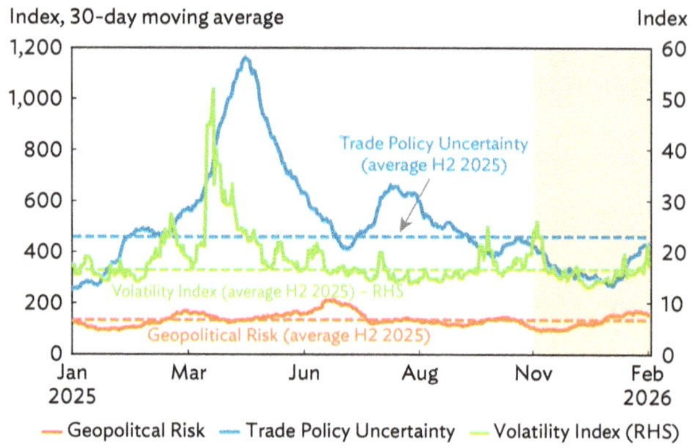


H2 = second half, RHS = right-hand side.

Note: Data as of 6 February 2026.

Source: Bloomberg LP, Geopolitical Risk Index, and Trade Policy Uncertainty Index (accessed 18 February 2026); Caldara, D. et al. 2020. The Economic Effects of Trade Policy Uncertainty. *Journal of Monetary Economics*. 109. pp. 38–59; Caldara, D., and M. Iacoviello. 2022. Measuring Geopolitical Risk. *American Economic Review*. April. 112 (4). pp. 1194–1225.

friction between the US and European Union economies, which receded after a reversal in the US tariff stance was announced on 21 January in Davos, Switzerland. Afterward, a series of negative events—including a market rout fueled by AI and technology-sector valuation concerns and the possibility of the Fed restarting quantitative tightening—generated risk-off sentiment among investors, leading to another spike in volatility.

Bond yields in advanced economies climbed during the review period. Yields in the euro area rose largely due to the European Central Bank's (ECB) wait-and-see stance. In Japan, yields inched up on rising expectations of rate hikes and expansionary fiscal policy. Bond yields in the US rose amid concerns that the Fed might revert to quantitative tightening.

## United States

The US saw its 10-year yield rise between 3 November 2025 and 6 February 2026 over the Fed's more hawkish-than-expected stance. The 2-year yield declined during the review period, mostly driven by an expected December rate cut and supportive financial conditions following the end of the Fed's quantitative tightening on 1 December, which was announced during the October meeting. The Fed gradually shifted toward a cautious stance, as evidenced by the December Federal Open Market Committee (FOMC) meeting's statement about "considering the extent and timing of additional adjustments." The December FOMC meeting minutes showed that some members who voted for a rate cut could have also supported keeping rates unchanged. At the 28–29 January FOMC meeting, the Fed held the policy rate steady and noted that unemployment had stabilized. On 30 January, Kevin Warsh was nominated to be the next Fed chair, which briefly sparked market expectations that the Fed might resume quantitative tightening. During the review period, the market was still expecting a cumulative 50 basis points (bps) rate cut by the end of 2026, as measured by the CME FedWatch tool (**Figure B**).

**Figure B: Daily Probability of Year-End Federal Reserve Target Rate Range**

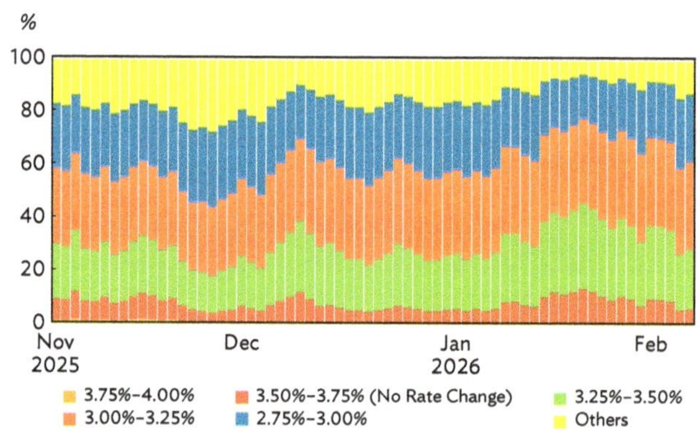


Notes:
1. Data are as of 6 February 2026.
2. Others reflect probabilities of four rate cuts or more.

Source: CME FedWatch Tool.

US economic performance rebounded during the review period, with softening yet still above-target inflation and a stabilizing job market. US final third quarter (Q3) annualized gross domestic product (GDP) growth was revised up to 4.4% from 4.3% (second estimate), an improvement from the previous quarter's 3.8%. However, Q4 2025 GDP growth slowed to 1.4%, dragged by the government shutdown, which ended on 12 November. Industrial production posted consecutive gains of 0.7% month-on-month (m-o-m) in January, 0.3% m-o-m in December and 0.1% m-o-m in November, following a decline of 0.3% m-o-m in October. The S&P Global Manufacturing Purchasing Managers' Index (PMI) remained in expansionary territory at 51.2 in February, 52.4 in January, 51.8 in December, and 52.2 in November. The Fed noted that growth could strengthen in the first quarter of 2026 following the reopening of government operations after the shutdown. In December, the Fed revised upward its GDP forecasts for 2026 and 2027 to 2.3% and 2.0%, respectively, from projections of 1.8% and 1.9% made in September.

Inflation softened but remained above the Fed's 2.0% target. Inflation fell steadily to 2.4% year-on-year (y-o-y) in January and 2.7% y-o-y in December and November from 3.0% y-o-y in September. However, Personal Consumption Expenditures inflation, which lags consumer price data, remained persistent at 2.9% y-o-y in December, 2.8% y-o-y in November, and 2.7% y-o-y in October, compared to 2.8% in September. In December, the Fed projected that inflation would continue to soften, revising downward its forecasts for 2025 and 2026 to 2.9% and 2.4%, respectively, from forecasts of 3.0% and 2.6% made in September.

The US job market remained weak with signs of stabilization during the review period. Nonfarm payroll additions recorded a higher-than-expected 130,000 in January, up from a revised 48,000 in December and 41,000 in November. The unemployment rate inched down slightly to 4.3% in January from 4.4% in December and 4.5% in November. Nevertheless, downward revisions to 2025 nonfarm payroll data showed that the labor market was weaker than previously thought as total nonfarm payrolls additions in 2025 were revised down to 181,000 from 584,000. Moreover, the December Job Openings and Labor Turnover Survey number of 6.5 million, released on 5 February, was lower than both the expected 7.3 million job openings and November's reading of 6.9 million, which was previously the lowest level since October 2020. The Fed kept its unemployment forecast for 2026 at 4.4% in December, the same as its September projection, and revised downward the 2027 forecast to 4.2% from September's 4.3%.

## Euro Area

The 2-year and 10-year bond yields in the euro area—proxied by Bloomberg's Euro Generic Government Bond Yields—rose strongly during the review period, driven by the ECB's wait-and-see monetary stance, a stabilized and resilient economic outlook, and the planned increase in Germany's federal spending in 2026.[3] The ECB maintained its wait-and-see stance and left policy rates unchanged at its December 2025 and February 2026 meetings over resilient GDP growth in the euro area. While growth fell slightly to 1.3% y-o-y in Q4 2025 from 1.4% y-o-y in Q3 2025, q-o-q growth remained unchanged at 0.3% and exceeded the ECB's forecast for Q4 2025 of 0.2% q-o-q. Inflation in the euro area eased to 1.7% y-o-y in January and 2.0% y-o-y in December from 2.1% y-o-y in October and November. The unemployment rate also declined, with December unemployment coming in at 6.2% versus 6.3% in November and October. The HCOB Manufacturing PMI stabilized at around the 50.0 threshold during the review period, with readings of 50.8 in February, 49.5 in January, 48.8 in December, and 49.6 in November—compared with 50.0 in October.

The ECB acknowledged that economic growth was resilient and inflation was stabilizing around its target, while also noting greater uncertainty regarding the inflation outlook due to global headwinds, largely around trade. At the December meeting, the ECB revised its GDP forecasts for 2026 and 2027 upward to 1.2% and 1.4%, respectively, from September's projections of 1.0% and 1.3%. The ECB raised its inflation forecast for 2026 to 1.9% from 1.7% in September and lowered the forecast for 2027 to 1.8% from 1.9% in September. At the February meeting, the ECB announced that it expected inflation to settle around the central bank's target over the medium-term.

## Japan

The 2-year and 10-year yields in Japan rose during the review period amid increased hawkishness from the Bank of Japan (BOJ) as well as expectations of an expansionary fiscal policy. The BOJ raised the policy rate by 25 bps at its 18–19 December meeting, as it expected that wages and prices would continue to rise. The BOJ also implied additional rate hikes would follow on the condition that its October 2025 forecasts for the economic outlook were met. The hawkish tone was affirmed in the BOJ's Summary of Opinions released on 29 December. In the summary, the BOJ noted that (i) current market conditions were a partial reflection of its policy rate being too low relative to inflation, and (ii) further interest rate hikes could help reduce future inflationary pressure. The BOJ left its policy rate on hold at its 22–23 January

[3] On 14 November, the German Bundestag's Budget Committee revealed its 2026 budget plan, showing an increase in net debt of EUR98 billion, up from EUR90 billion in a previous proposal. If funding for defense and infrastructure is included, net debt is expected to increase by EUR180 billion. The budget plan was later signed into law on 28 November.

meeting, with its updated forecasts showing that the economy is expected to grow as external demand improves and prices remain elevated.

Japan's economic performance rebounded but remained subdued, while inflation continued to decline but remained above target. Though weaker than expected, Japan's GDP growth recovered to an annualized 0.2% in Q4 2025 after declining 2.3% in Q3 2025, driven by domestic consumption and investment. Industrial production contracted in December (–0.1% m-o-m) and November (–2.7% m-o-m). Consumer price inflation continued to decelerate, moderating to 1.5% y-o-y in January from 2.1% y-o-y in December, 2.9% y-o-y in November, and 3.0% y-o-y in October. When excluding fresh food and energy, consumer price inflation stood at 2.6% y-o-y in January, 2.9% y-o-y in December, and 3.0% y-o-y in November, down from 3.1% y-o-y in October.

To support economic performance, Prime Minister Sanae Takaichi announced plans for tax cuts, including a 2-year temporary suspension of the consumption tax on food. In December, the Japanese National Diet passed a JPY18.3 trillion supplementary budget for fiscal year 2025. The victory of the Prime Minister's party in the 8 February elections reinforced market expectations of an expansionary fiscal stance. Japan's business sentiment improved, with the Manufacturing PMI reaching 53.0 in February—its highest level since May 2022—and 51.5 in January, up from 50.0 in December and 48.7 in November. In January, the BOJ upgraded its GDP growth forecasts to 0.9% for fiscal year 2025 and 1.0% for fiscal year 2026, from 0.7% for both in October. The BOJ also raised its consumer price inflation forecast for fiscal year 2026 to 1.9% from 1.8% in October. For consumer price inflation excluding fresh food and energy, the forecast for fiscal year 2026 was raised to 2.2% from 2.0% in October.

## Emerging East Asia

In emerging East Asian bond markets, 10-year yields collectively rose during the review period on yield upticks in major advanced economies and market-specific factors. Some regional economies witnessed a modest increase in inflation—but still within their respective central bank targets (**Figure C**). This allowed regional central banks to maintain accommodative monetary stances, with the Philippines and Thailand cutting interest rates in December 2025 (**Table B**). The Bangko Sentral ng Pilipinas, as expected, again cut its policy rate by 25 bps on 19 February to support the weakening economy. The 2-year yield declined in most emerging East Asian bond markets—tracking the 2-year yield's movement in the US—amid accommodative monetary policies from regional central banks. Bucking regional trends, 2-year bond yields rose in the Republic of Korea, Viet Nam, and Indonesia on market-specific factors:

- Bond yields rose in the Republic of Korea over a hawkish shift by the Bank of Korea (BOK) and the possibility of an increase in government spending. At its 27 November meeting, the BOK left its policy

**Figure C: Inflation in Major Advanced Economies and Select Emerging East Asian Markets**

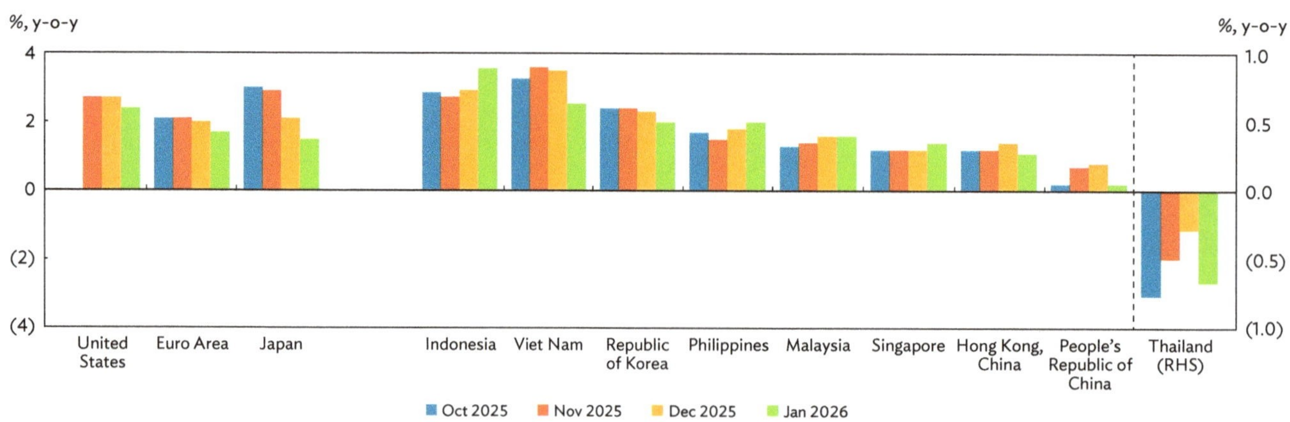


( ) = negative, RHS = right-hand side, y-o-y = year-on-year.
Note: For the United States, inflation data were not available for October 2025.
Sources: Various local sources.

**Table B: Changes in Monetary Stances in Major Advanced Economies and Select Emerging East Asian Markets**

| Economy | Policy Rate 1-Feb-2025 (%) | Rate Change (%) Feb-2025 | Mar-2025 | Apr-2025 | May-2025 | Jun-2025 | Jul-2025 | Aug-2025 | Sep-2025 | Oct-2025 | Nov-2025 | Dec-2025 | Jan-2026 | Feb-2026 | Policy Rate 6-Feb-2026 (%) | Change in Policy Rates (basis points) |
|---|---|---|---|---|---|---|---|---|---|---|---|---|---|---|---|---|
| Euro Area | 3.00 | ↓0.25 | ↓0.25 | ↓0.25 | | ↓0.25 | | | | | | | | | 2.00 | ↓ 100 |
| Japan | 0.50 | | | | | | | | | | | ↑0.25 | | | 0.75 | ↑ 25 |
| United Kingdom | 4.75 | ↓0.25 | | | ↓0.25 | | | ↓0.25 | | | | ↓0.25 | | | 3.75 | ↓ 100 |
| United States | 4.50 | | | | | | | | ↓0.25 | ↓0.25 | | ↓0.25 | | | 3.75 | ↓ 75 |
| People's Republic of China | 1.50 | | | | ↓0.10 | | | | | | | | | | 1.40 | ↓ 10 |
| Indonesia | 5.75 | | | | ↓0.25 | | ↓0.25 | ↓0.25 | ↓0.25 | | | | | | 4.75 | ↓ 100 |
| Republic of Korea | 3.00 | ↓0.25 | | | ↓0.25 | | | | | | | | | | 2.50 | ↓ 50 |
| Malaysia | 3.00 | | | | | | ↓0.25 | | | | | | | | 2.75 | ↓ 25 |
| Philippines | 5.75 | | | ↓0.25 | | ↓0.25 | | ↓0.25 | | ↓0.25 | | ↓0.25 | | | 4.50 | ↓ 125 |
| Singapore | – | | | ↓ | | | | | | | | | | | – | ↓ – |
| Thailand | 2.25 | ↓0.25 | | ↓0.25 | | | | ↓0.25 | | | | ↓0.25 | | | 1.25 | ↓ 100 |
| Viet Nam | 4.50 | | | | | | | | | | | | | | 4.50 | ◆ 0 |

– = no data.

Notes:
1. Data coverage is from 1 February 2025 to 6 February 2026.
2. For the People's Republic of China, the data used in the chart are for the 7-day reverse repurchase rate.
3. For the United States, the upper bound of the policy rate target range is reported on the table.
4. An arrow up (down) indicates a policy rate hike (cut). A diamond indicates no change in the policy rate.
5. For Singapore, the up (down) arrow signifies monetary policy tightening (loosening) by its central bank. The Monetary Authority of Singapore utilizes the Singapore dollar nominal effective exchange rate to guide its monetary policy.

Sources: Various central bank websites.

rate unchanged and removed previous language about "maintaining a rate cut stance." The BOK also noted that recent inflation has been higher than expected. In both January and February, the government hinted that another supplemental budget might be passed in the first half of 2026.

- Yields in Viet Nam increased over an expanded bond issuance plan in 2026—with scheduled issuances totaling VND500.0 trillion, up from VND371.5 trillion in 2025.
- Indonesian yields rose on market stress in January when MSCI warned of the potential reduction of Indonesian stock weights in its MSCI Emerging Market Index or a possible downgrade of Indonesia's classification to the Frontier Market Index.[4] Investors were also concerned about the government's fiscal stance as the 2025 budget deficit reached 2.9% of GDP, nearly hitting the legal debt limit of 3.0%. In addition, Moody's Ratings downgraded Indonesia's sovereign credit outlook from "stable" to "negative" on 5 February, further pushing up bond yields. On 9 February, FTSE Russell announced that it will delay its March 2026 planned review of Indonesian stocks.

The region saw resilient economic performance in Q4 2025, with growth accelerating in six out of nine markets compared with Q3 2025 (**Table C**). Singapore's Q4 2025 GDP expanded 6.9% y-o-y, up from 4.6% y-o-y in Q3 2025, amid a manufacturing boom led by AI-fueled demand. Thailand recorded Q4 GDP growth of 2.5% y-o-y, accelerating from 1.2% y-o-y in Q3 2025 over strong domestic consumption, investment, and government spending. Malaysia posted Q4 2025 GDP growth of 6.3% y-o-y, up from 5.4% y-o-y in Q3 2025, boosted by expansions in services and manufacturing and rising domestic demand. Viet Nam again had the strongest GDP performance in the region with a Q4 2025 growth rate of 8.5% y-o-y, up from 8.3% y-o-y in the previous quarter, driven by continued government efforts to boost the economy. Meanwhile, the People's Republic of China's (PRC) Q4 2025 growth was within expectations at 4.5% y-o-y, while its full-year 2025 GDP growth of 5.0% met the government's target. The Republic of Korea experienced slower Q4 2025 GDP growth of 1.5% y-o-y, compared with 1.8% y-o-y in Q3 2025, mostly due to weaker domestic demand. The Philippines experienced the region's biggest slowdown, with Q4 2025 growth falling

[4] MSCI flagged transparency issues related to equity share ownership structures and the quality of available free float data in the Indonesian market.

**Table C: Gross Domestic Product Growth in Select Emerging East Asian Economies** (y-o-y, %)

| Economy | 2025 Q1 | 2025 Q2 | 2025 Q3 | 2025 Q4 | 2025 Full Year | Forecast for Full Year 2025 |
|---|---|---|---|---|---|---|
| PRC | 5.40 | 5.20 | 4.80 | 4.50 | 5.00 | 4.80 |
| HKG | 3.10 | 3.20 | 3.70 | 3.80 | 3.50 | 3.40 |
| INO | 4.87 | 5.12 | 5.04 | 5.39 | 5.11 | 5.00 |
| ROK | 0.00 | 0.60 | 1.80 | 1.50 | 1.00 | 0.90 |
| MAL | 4.40 | 4.40 | 5.40 | 6.30 | 5.20 | 4.50 |
| PHI | 5.40 | 5.50 | 3.95 | 3.00 | 4.40 | 5.00 |
| SIN | 3.90 | 4.60 | 4.60 | 6.90 | 5.00 | 4.10 |
| THA | 3.20 | 2.80 | 1.20 | 2.50 | 2.40 | 2.00 |
| VIE | 7.05 | 8.16 | 8.25 | 8.46 | 8.02 | 7.40 |

PRC = People's Republic of China; HKG = Hong Kong, China; INO = Indonesia; ROK = Republic of Korea; MAL = Malaysia; PHI = Philippines; Q1 = first quarter; Q2 = second quarter; Q3 = third quarter; Q4 = fourth quarter; SIN = Singapore; THA = Thailand; VIE = Viet Nam; y-o-y = year-on-year.

Notes:
1. Forecasts for 2025 are based on the *Asian Development Outlook December 2025*.
2. Q4 2025 and full year data for the Republic of Korea are based on advanced estimates.

Sources: Various local sources.

to 3.0% y-o-y from 4.0% y-o-y in Q3 2025, amid a slump in private consumption growth and reduced government construction spending.

Risk premiums, measured by credit default swap (CDS) spreads, diverged across the region during the review period on market-specific patterns. Risk premiums widened in most regional markets in November 2025 and January 2026, reflecting heightened risk aversion (**Figure D**). In November, CDS spreads rose in nearly all markets on increased volatility due to receding expectations of a December rate cut by the Fed and concerns about the overvaluation of AI technology stocks. CDS spread movements subsequently reversed, narrowing in December following the Fed rate cut and as concerns over a potential AI bubble eased. In January, however, CDS spreads rose again in several markets, most notably in Indonesia (7.7 bps) on market stress related to MSCI's review and in the Philippines (2.4 bps) after it reported weak growth in Q4 2025 GDP. Viet Nam registered the region's largest decline in the CDS spread (−9.1 bps) in January amid strong economic growth and Fitch Ratings' upgrade of its senior secured long-term debt to BB+ from BBB−. In February, regional markets saw their respective CDS spreads diverge. Indonesia's spread widened further following the downgrade from Moody's Ratings, while Viet Nam's rose following the release of January's trade balance data, which showed the largest deficit since February 2022 despite expectations of a surplus. Meanwhile, Malaysia's CDS spread narrowed over an improving growth outlook.

**Figure D: Changes in Credit Default Swap Spreads in Select Emerging East Asian Markets** (senior 5-year)

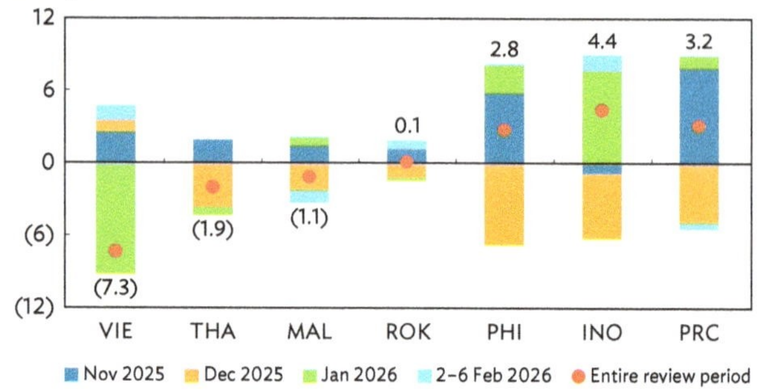


( ) = negative; PRC = People's Republic of China; INO = Indonesia; ROK = Republic of Korea; MAL = Malaysia; PHI = Philippines; THA = Thailand; VIE = Viet Nam.

Note: The numbers above (below) each bar refer to the change in spreads between 3 November 2025 and 6 February 2026.

Source: *AsianBondsOnline* calculations based on Bloomberg LP data.

Equity markets gained in most regional economies during the review period, bolstered by strong economic growth in Q4 2025 and the ongoing AI boom. Regional stocks gained 4.2% (market-weighted average) (**Figure E**). AI stocks lifted equity performances across the region, with the biggest jump recorded in the Republic of Korea (20.5%), driven by its semiconductor industry. Singapore's

**Figure E: Changes in Equity Indexes in Select Emerging East Asian Markets**

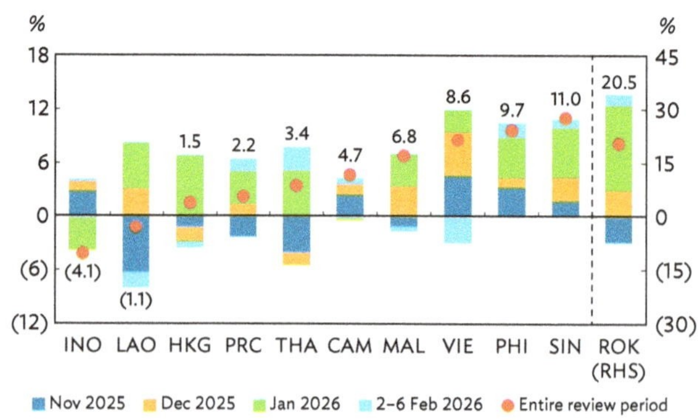


( ) = negative; CAM = Cambodia; PRC = People's Republic of China; HKG = Hong Kong, China; INO = Indonesia; ROK = Republic of Korea; LAO = Lao People's Democratic Republic; MAL = Malaysia; PHI = Philippines; RHS = right-hand side; SIN = Singapore; THA = Thailand; VIE = Viet Nam.

Note: The numbers above (below) each bar refer to the percentage change between 3 November 2025 and 6 February 2026.

Source: *AsianBondsOnline* calculations based on Bloomberg LP data.

equity market gained 11.0%, supported by strong Q4 2025 GDP growth and demand for semiconductor manufactures. The Philippine market rose 9.7% over news that the government would spend PHP1.4 billion in the first quarter of 2026 to support economic growth. Viet Nam's equity market rose 8.6% on optimism over regulatory reforms to support Viet Nam's inclusion in FTSE Russell's emerging market index by September 2026. Only Indonesia posted equity losses (–4.1%) during the review period, as its gains in earlier months were more than offset by a market rout following MSCI's review in January. Emerging East Asia saw equity losses in November (–2.1%, market-weighted average) over a market sell-off driven by AI valuation concerns. Markets subsequently recovered in December–January, supported by the Fed's December rate cut and an upturn in AI-related sentiment.

Most regional equity markets recorded net inflows during the review period as resilient economic fundamentals helped weather global market volatility. Four out of six regional markets with available data recorded portfolio inflows. The PRC and the Republic of Korea experienced both large inflows and outflows over the course of the review period, tracking the shifts in AI-valuation concerns (**Figure F**). These capital flows were mainly driven by risk sentiment related to tech stocks. The region saw net outflows of USD23.2 billion in November, largely due to a sell-off amid concerns over tech stock valuations, with particularly notable outflows from the PRC (–USD13.6 billion) and the Republic of Korea (–USD9.7 billion). In December, equity flows turned positive on the recovery in investor sentiment surrounding AI and the Fed's rate cut. In January, improved growth sentiment in the region and strong corporate earnings generated additional inflows, with the PRC witnessing inflows of USD24.4 billion. February saw regional outflows of USD22.1 billion, led by the PRC and the Republic of Korea, over more AI related sell-offs. Excluding the Republic of Korea, the region saw net equity inflows of USD2.1 billion during the review period.

Regional bond markets logged net portfolio inflows of USD12.2 billion in November–January, largely due to an improved growth outlook for most markets in the region. Easing inflation in the US led to increased expectations of a rate cut in December, which contributed to bond inflows in emerging East Asia. Among regional bond markets, the Republic of Korea posted the largest net portfolio inflows of USD19.2 billion, as investors ramped up their holdings ahead of the Republic of Korea's inclusion in the FTSE Russell World Government Bond Index in April 2026 (**Figure G**). In contrast, the PRC posted net portfolio

**Figure F: Foreign Capital Flows in Select Emerging East Asian Equity Markets**

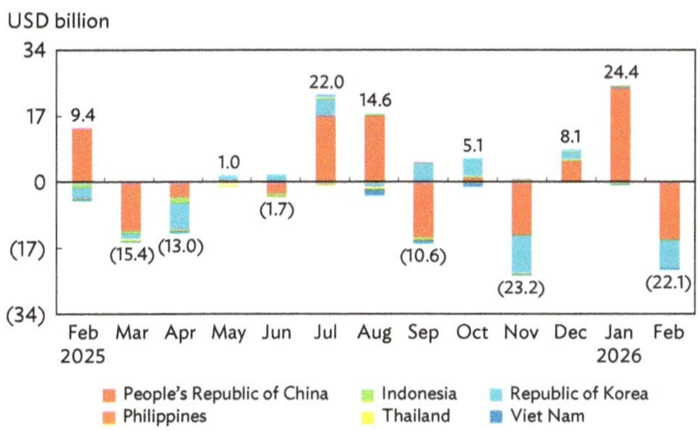


( ) = negative, USD = United States dollar.

Notes:
1. Data coverage is from 1 February 2025 to 6 February 2026.
2. The numbers above (below) each bar refer to net inflows (net outflows) for each month.
3. Emerging East Asia is defined to include member states of the Association of Southeast Asian Nations (ASEAN) plus the People's Republic of China; Hong Kong, China; and the Republic of Korea.

Source: Institute of International Finance.

**Figure G: Foreign Capital Flows in Select Emerging East Asian Local Currency Bond Markets**

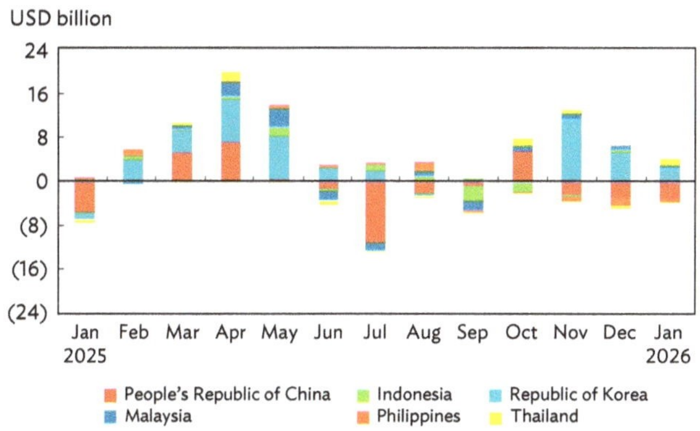


( ) = negative, USD = United States dollar.

Notes:
1. The Republic of Korea and Thailand provided data on bond flows. For the People's Republic of China, Indonesia, Malaysia, and the Philippines, month-on-month changes in foreign holdings of local currency government bonds were used as a proxy for bond flows.
2. Data are as of 31 January 2026.
3. Figures were computed based on 31 January 2026 exchange rates and do not include currency effects.

Sources: People's Republic of China (Bloomberg LP); Indonesia (Directorate General of Budget Financing and Risk Management, Ministry of Finance); Republic of Korea (Financial Supervisory Service); Malaysia (Bank Negara Malaysia); Philippines (Bureau of the Treasury); and Thailand (Thai Bond Market Association).

outflows of USD8.3 billion in November–January over investor concerns amid slow economic growth. Meanwhile, the Philippines experienced USD2.6 billion of net outflows following successive rate cuts in August, October, December, and February.

Emerging East Asian currencies appreciated against the US dollar by 1.3% (simple average) and 2.0% (GDP-weighted) during the review period due to a rate cut and heightened uncertainty in the US and the region's resilient economic performance (**Figure H**). Regional currencies strengthened in December, following the US rate cut, and again in January, when rising geopolitical tensions led to the depreciation of the US dollar. During the review period, the Malaysian ringgit posted the region's largest gain of 6.4% over improved investor sentiment and the government's fiscal consolidation plan. Meanwhile, the Korean won depreciated 2.2% against the US dollar on strong domestic dollar demand for the US dollar, including the purchasing of US stocks by retail investors. The Indonesian rupiah depreciated 1.2% against the US dollar, largely due to portfolio outflows following a market sell-off in January.

**Figure H: Currency Exchange Rates Against the United States Dollar in Select Emerging East Asian Markets**

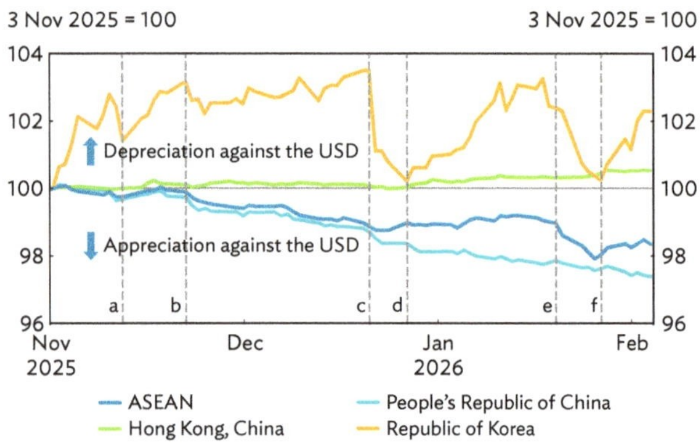


ASEAN = Association of Southeast Asian Nations, USD = United States dollar.

Notes:

1. Corresponding dates of the following events:
   - a Growing number of Fed officials signal reticence on further easing.
   - b Dovish remark from New York Fed President John Williams about a rate cut at the December Federal Open Market Committee meeting.
   - c Heightened geopolitical tensions drive investors away from the USD.
   - d Korean won depreciates amid strong domestic demand for the USD.
   - e Planned US tariffs for European economies were pulled back.
   - f Kevin Warsh is expected to replace Fed Chair Jerome Powell in May, raising market concerns that the Fed might resume quantitative tightening.
2. ASEAN comprises the markets of Brunei Darussalam, Cambodia, Indonesia, the Lao People's Democratic Republic, Malaysia, the Philippines, Singapore, Thailand, and Viet Nam.
3. Data are as of 6 February 2026.
4. An increase (decrease) in the value indicates depreciation (appreciation) of the currency against the USD.

Source: *AsianBondsOnline* calculations based on Bloomberg LP data.

Regional financial markets are expected to remain broadly resilient as upside and downside risks appear balanced. On the upside, the region's generally solid macroeconomic fundamentals and accommodative monetary policies should help cushion external shocks. If the AI-related investment cycle continues to gain momentum and productivity gains materialize, sustained earnings growth in the technology sector could reinforce equity market performance, support capital inflows, and strengthen broader market sentiment across the region.

Meanwhile, several downside risks warrant close monitoring. The prolonged property sector downturn in the PRC remains a significant risk to regional growth and financial stability. New home prices across 70 cities fell 2.7% y-o-y in December 2025, accelerating from a 2.4% y-o-y decline in November. S&P Global Ratings recently downgraded its outlook, projecting property sales to drop by about 10%–14% in 2026, compared with earlier expectations of a 5%–8% decline. Continued weakness could dampen domestic demand, weigh on fiscal finances, and constrain credit expansion. Abrupt changes in investor sentiment, especially AI-related concerns, could lead to spikes in market volatility. The VIX Index and tech stocks' performance have shown a highly negative correlation (**Figure I**). Uncertainty about the US monetary policy path—including the upcoming leadership transition at the Fed, the pace of future interest rate adjustments, and possible quantitative tightening—could contribute to fluctuations in asset prices and global capital flows. **Box 1** highlights how improved policy frameworks and the development of local currency bond markets enhance financial resilience in emerging markets, including in ASEAN markets.

**Figure I: Tech Stock Market Performance and Chicago Board Options Exchange Volatility Index**

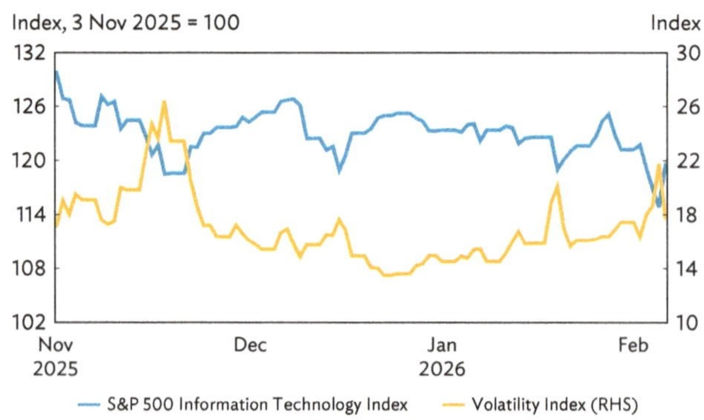


RHS = right-hand side.

Note: Data are as of 6 February 2026.

Source: Bloomberg, LP.

Unexpected trade policy and geopolitical developments could also heighten uncertainty. Rising trade fragmentation poses both risks and opportunities for regional financial markets. On the downside, increased tariffs, export controls, and policy uncertainty can weigh on export-oriented sectors and heighten earnings volatility for firms integrated into global value chains, potentially leading to capital flow volatility and weaker investor sentiment. At the same time, economies that benefit from supply chain diversification and "friend-shoring" trends could attract increased foreign direct investment and portfolio inflows, supporting domestic financial conditions.

## Box 1: Building Resilience in Emerging Market Local Currency Bond Markets

**Improved policy frameworks and the development of local currency (LCY) bond markets have strengthened financial resilience in emerging markets, including in Asia.** Emerging markets historically face higher financial stability risks when they borrow in foreign currency and when nonresident investors hold a large share of domestic debt. Increased LCY debt issuance to domestic investors in recent years has reduced both currency mismatches and the risk of sudden capital outflows.[a]

**Improvements in financial stability remain uneven across economies, and government debt has increased sharply since 2010.** LCY bond market development lags in many developing economies, including in parts of Asia with lingering structural constraints. Strong macroeconomic frameworks and subdued inflation and exchange rate volatility have enabled major Asian emerging markets to primarily issue in local currency, particularly for longer-term fixed-rate bonds, including *sukuk* (Islamic bonds) (**Figure B1.1**). However, many smaller emerging markets and frontier markets still rely significantly on foreign currency issuance, short-term LCY debt, or concessional lending. Among frontier markets, Asian economies rely relatively more on LCY debt but issue at shorter maturities.

### Investor Composition

**Nonresident investor participation in LCY debt has fallen to multiyear lows across most emerging markets.**[b] While a few markets experienced large outflows of LCY debt from 2012 to 2024, nonresident inflows generally stagnated and failed to keep pace with heavy domestic issuance (**Figure B1.2**). Risk-adjusted returns for this asset class were poor for much of the last decade, partially due to the persistent strength of the dollar prior to 2025. Nonresident participation is broadly lower across emerging markets in

**Figure B1.1: Local Currency Bond Market Composition in Emerging Markets**

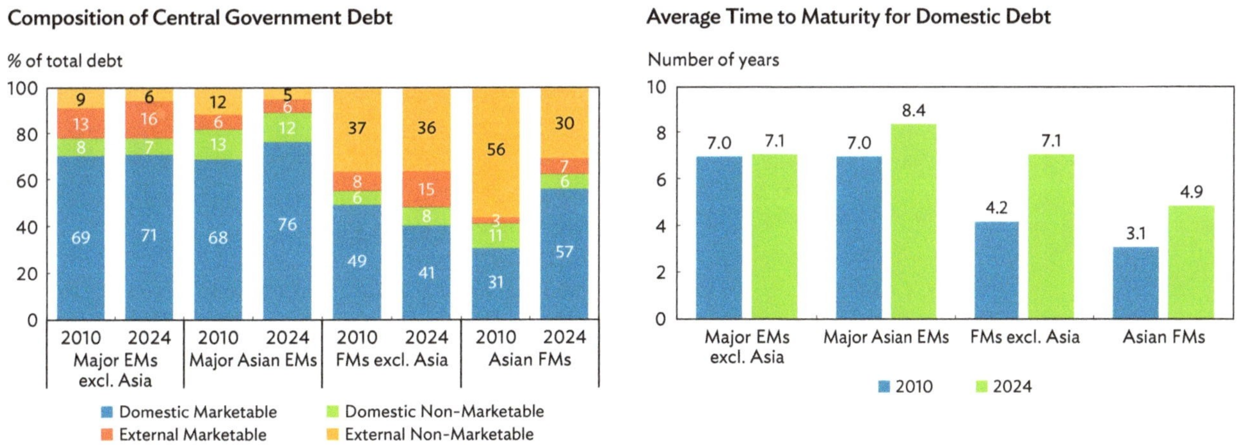


EM = emerging market, FM = frontier market.

Source: International Monetary Fund. 2025. *Global Financial Stability Report, October 2025.* https://www.imf.org/en/publications/gfsr/issues/2025/10/14/global-financial-stability-report-october-2025.

*continued on next page*

## Box 1 *continued*

**Figure B1.2: Local Currency Bond Market Investor Composition in Emerging Markets**

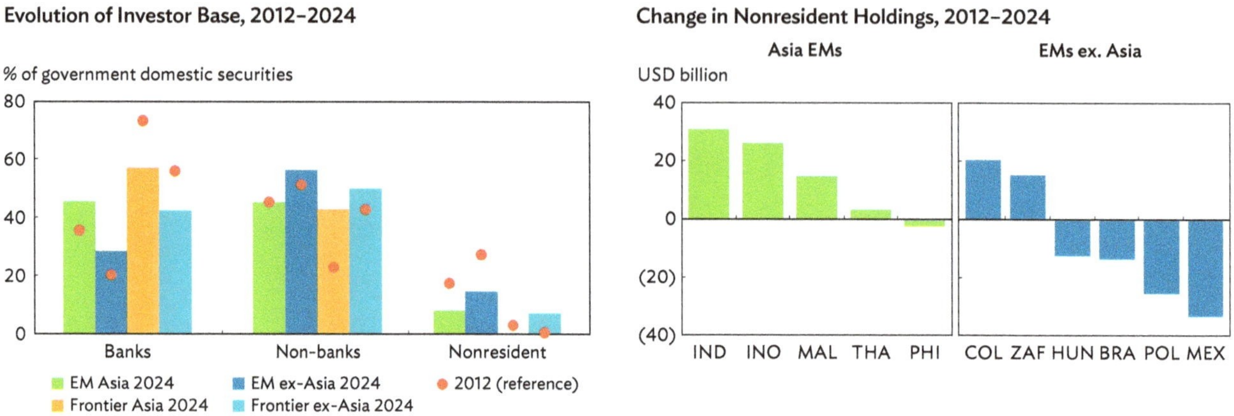


( ) = negative, BRA = Brazil, COL = Colombia, EM = emerging market, HUN = Hungary, IND = India, INO = Indonesia, MAL = Malaysia, MEX = Mexico, PHI = Philippines, POL = Poland, THA = Thailand, USD = United States dollar, ZAF = South Africa.

Source: International Monetary Fund. 2025. *Global Financial Stability Report*, October 2025. https://www.imf.org/en/publications/gfsr/issues/2025/10/14/global-financial-stability-report-october-2025.

Asia compared to emerging markets in other regions, though nonresidents hold about 20% of LCY debt in Malaysia. Among frontier markets, nonresident ownership varies greatly, with some economies prone to large capital flow cycles (e.g., Egypt, Ghana), while nonresident ownership in others is negligible.

**Banks continue to play a dominant role in absorbing domestic issuance, though nonbank financial institutions (NBFIs) are increasing their purchases of LCY debt in some emerging markets.** In major Asian emerging markets, the domestic investor composition remains balanced between banks and NBFIs. Elsewhere, NBFIs have generally increased their market share over the last decade, with NBFI ownership exceeding banks in some cases. In contrast, many frontier markets remain highly dependent on banks, particularly across Asia. Several emerging markets outside of Asia have more developed NBFI sectors with sizeable pension and investment fund assets, notably in South Africa, Brazil, and Chile.[c]

**Greater domestic ownership reduces the sensitivity of emerging market LCY bond markets to global shocks.** Empirical analysis of data covering 2012–2024 shows that a shock of 10 percentage points in the Volatility Index increases LCY bond yields by about 19 basis points (Chen et al. 2025). A higher share of domestic bank ownership—one standard deviation above average—reduces the impact to about 11 basis points. Greater nonresident ownership increases the impact to 23 basis points. For domestic NBFIs, the results are more nuanced, but any positive effect appears more significant for pension funds and insurance companies, which have long-term investment horizons. Model results for liquidity, proxied by bid–ask spreads, show similar patterns. However, higher levels of domestic bond ownership also have drawbacks. LCY bond markets with limited absorption capacity are more prone to risks from the increasing sovereign–bank nexus. Policymakers also may resort to financial repression to place debt at below-market rates.

### Market Functioning

**Market functioning matters for bond market resilience just as much as investor composition.** Government bond market liquidity in emerging markets lags advanced economies, though many markets have improved over time. The picture is mixed for Asian emerging markets. They tend to issue a larger number of smaller bond lines, while repo and hedging markets are less developed, which limits market depth. Bank trading books in major Asian emerging markets are typically smaller than in other major emerging markets, constraining dealers' ability to intermediate risk and reducing turnover. For pre-trades on benchmark bonds, firm-price availability is universal across emerging markets, and bid–ask spreads in major Asian emerging markets are as tight as in other major emerging markets. In frontier markets, average trade sizes are significantly smaller with shallow liquidity.

*continued on next page*

## Box 1 *continued*

### Policy Framework

**LCY bond market development forms part of a broader financial stability agenda.** Sovereign issuance is not just a financing tool; it is also about market building. Issuing debt at fair, market-clearing yields strengthens market discipline and helps policymakers act early when needed. A nonmarket approach to issuing government securities—characterized by administratively set yields, ad hoc interventions, price-making behavior, multiple instruments offered at each auction, and irregular auction management—fundamentally undermines price discovery and investor confidence.

**The LCY bond market framework of the International Monetary Fund (IMF) and the World Bank prioritizes six core policy areas for reform**: (i) money market, (ii) primary market, (iii) secondary market, (iv) investor base, (v) financial market infrastructure, and (vi) legal and regulatory framework. These pillars provide a clear structure for economies aiming to deepen their markets to support stable domestic financing, strengthen policy transmission, and remain functional even under global stress. The IMF and World Bank provide programmatic technical assistance on LCY bond market development to members, supported by capacity building through the IMF's online training module on LCY bond market development.

### References

Chen, S., et al. 2025. Chapter 3: Global Shocks, Local Markets: The Changing Landscape of Emerging Market Sovereign Debt. In *Global Financial Stability Report, October 2025*. IMF. pp. 77–103.

IMF and World Bank. 2021. Analytical Note 2021/001: Guidance Note for Developing Government Local Currency Bond Markets. Washington, DC.

This box is based on © International Monetary Fund. 2025. *Global Financial Stability Report, October 2025*. https://www.imf.org/en/publications/gfsr/issues/2025/10/14/global-financial-stability-report-october-2025. It was written by Bryan Gurhy (senior financial sector expert), Arindam Roy (senior financial sector expert), Patrick Schneider (financial sector expert), and Xuege Zhang (economist), all from the Monetary and Capital Markets Department, IMF. The views expressed here are those of the authors and do not reflect the views of the IMF or its board.

[a] In this box, emerging markets comprise 12 economies, including 6 from Asia: the People's Republic of China, India, Indonesia, Malaysia, the Philippines, and Thailand. Frontier markets comprise 13 economies, including 4 from Asia: Armenia, Pakistan, Sri Lanka, and Viet Nam. Classification into major emerging markets and frontier markets is based on the size of the bond market (as a share of gross domestic product) and the size of individual bonds.

[b] Nonresident holdings increased in the People's Republic of China and India after policymakers relaxed foreign investment restrictions and LCY bonds were added to global benchmarks; however, their respective shares in total bonds remained low at the end of 2024.

[c] Among Asian emerging markets, Malaysia has a relatively deep NBFI sector. Pension and insurance allocations to government bonds are generally high in Asian emerging markets, partly reflecting their respective regulatory frameworks.

# Bond Market Developments in the Fourth Quarter of 2025

## Section 1. Local Currency Bonds Outstanding

**Emerging East Asian local currency (LCY) bonds outstanding reached USD30.6 trillion at the end of December 2025, with the market's expansion easing in the fourth quarter (Q4) as issuance declined from the previous quarter.**[5] The expansion of LCY bonds outstanding slowed to 2.1% quarter-on-quarter (q-o-q) in Q4 2025 from 3.2% q-o-q in the third quarter (Q3), as most regional governments had met their annual borrowing targets in earlier quarters (**Figure 1A**).

- Treasury and other government bonds outstanding in emerging East Asia totaled USD19.9 trillion at the end of December, accounting for 65.1% of the region's LCY bond stock. Government bonds outstanding expanded 2.0% q-o-q in Q4 2025, down from 3.7% q-o-q in the previous quarter, on reduced issuance as a majority of governments in the region had already fulfilled most of their annual borrowing needs in earlier quarters. The Philippines saw an uptick in its government bond stock due to a smaller volume of maturities. Viet Nam's government bonds outstanding expanded at an accelerated pace as the government continued issuance to meet its 2025 target.
- Corporate bonds outstanding (USD10.0 trillion) at the end of Q4 2025 comprised 32.7% of the region's total LCY bond market. The expansion of corporate bonds outstanding was broadly stable in Q4 2025, slowing marginally to 2.3% q-o-q from 2.5% q-o-q in the prior quarter. Viet Nam's corporate bonds outstanding rose 7.0% q-o-q, fueled by robust issuance as firms refinanced maturing debt. Expansion in most of the region's other corporate bond markets slowed from the previous quarter.
- The PRC remained the region's largest market, expanding 2.2% q-o-q to reach USD25.0 trillion at the end of Q4 2025 and accounting for 81.7% of the regional LCY bond stock (**Figure 1B**). This was followed by the Republic of Korea with a 7.9% share. ASEAN member economies' aggregate bond stock tallied USD2.7 trillion on expansion of 1.2% q-o-q, accounting for 8.8% of the region's total bond stock. Among ASEAN markets, Viet Nam made the largest contribution to the region's LCY bond market expansion in Q4 2025, with its bond stock surging 10.5% q-o-q to USD151.1 billion.
- LCY bonds outstanding as a percentage of gross domestic product (GDP) in emerging East Asia reached 115.8% at the end of Q4 2025, which was less than the corresponding percentages for the bond markets of the European Union 20 (EU-20) (134.2%) and the United States (US) (141.2%). The Republic of Korea and Malaysia led the region with the highest percentages of LCY bonds outstanding to GDP at 130.0% and 129.5%, respectively (**Figure 1C**).
- The size-weighted average tenor of Treasury bonds outstanding in emerging East Asia reached 9.1 years at the end of Q4 2025, exceeding that of the EU-20 (8.2 years) and the US (7.5 years). Around 53.9% of outstanding bonds in the region had remaining tenors of more than 5 years at the end of Q4 2025 (**Figure 1D**). In most ASEAN markets and the Republic of Korea, the share of Treasury bonds with remaining tenors longer than 10 years comprised over one-third of the total LCY bond stock. The size-weighted average tenor at the end of Q4 2025 was 13.8 years in the Republic of Korea and 9.4 years in ASEAN. Within ASEAN, Treasury bonds in Thailand and Singapore had the longest average tenors of 11.2 years and 9.9 years, respectively.

[5] Emerging East Asia is defined to include member states of the Association of Southeast Asian Nations plus the People's Republic of China; Hong Kong, China; and the Republic of Korea.

**Figure 1: Local Currency Bonds Outstanding in Emerging East Asian Markets**

ASEAN = Association of Southeast Asian Nations; PRC = People's Republic of China; EEA = emerging East Asia; EU-20 = European Union 20; GDP = gross domestic product; HKG = Hong Kong, China; INO = Indonesia; JPN = Japan; ROK = Republic of Korea; MAL = Malaysia; PHI = Philippines; RHS = right-hand side; Q1 = first quarter; Q2 = second quarter; Q3 = third quarter; Q4 = fourth quarter; SIN = Singapore; THA = Thailand; US = United States; USD = United States dollar; VIE = Viet Nam.

Notes:

1. Emerging East Asia is defined to include member states of the Association of Southeast Asian Nations plus the People's Republic of China; Hong Kong, China; and the Republic of Korea.
2. The EU-20 includes the member markets of Austria, Belgium, Croatia, Cyprus, Estonia, Finland, France, Germany, Greece, Ireland, Italy, Latvia, Lithuania, Luxembourg, Malta, the Netherlands, Portugal, Slovakia, Slovenia, and Spain.
3. Gross domestic product data for Q4 2025 are carried over from Q3 2025 for the Republic of Korea and the US.

Source: *AsianBondsOnline* calculations based on various local market sources.

**Treasury bonds outstanding in emerging East Asia at the end of Q4 2025 were mainly held by banks (Figure 2).** Banking institutions held 35.7% of outstanding Treasuries in the region, with notable increases in Indonesia, where banks' holdings rose to 20.2% at the end of 2025 from 17.4% a year earlier as foreign investors withdrew from the market. In the PRC, banks' holding share increased to 69.2% from 66.6% during the same period as demand for bank loans weakened. **Box 2** shows that systemic risk from growing bank–insurer interconnectedness is a tail phenomenon, intensifying sharply during extreme market conditions. Policymakers should focus on extremes—not averages—to safeguard financial stability. Strengthening market structures can help mitigate such risks by building a resilient LCY bond market. Insurance companies and pension funds were the second-largest investors in regional Treasury bonds in Q4 2025, holding 29.2% of the region's outstanding Treasuries, similar to their 29.1% share a year earlier. Meanwhile, the holdings share of foreign investors fell slightly to 10.7% from 10.8%, central banks' holding share dropped to 5.5% from 5.8%, while mutual funds' share dipped to 2.2% from 2.4%. These shifts contributed to increased investor concentration in the emerging East Asian Treasury bond market, as evidenced by a higher Herfindahl–Hirschman Index score in Q4 2025 compared with a year earlier.[6]

**Figure 2: Investor Profiles of Local Currency Treasury Bonds in Select Emerging East Asian Markets**

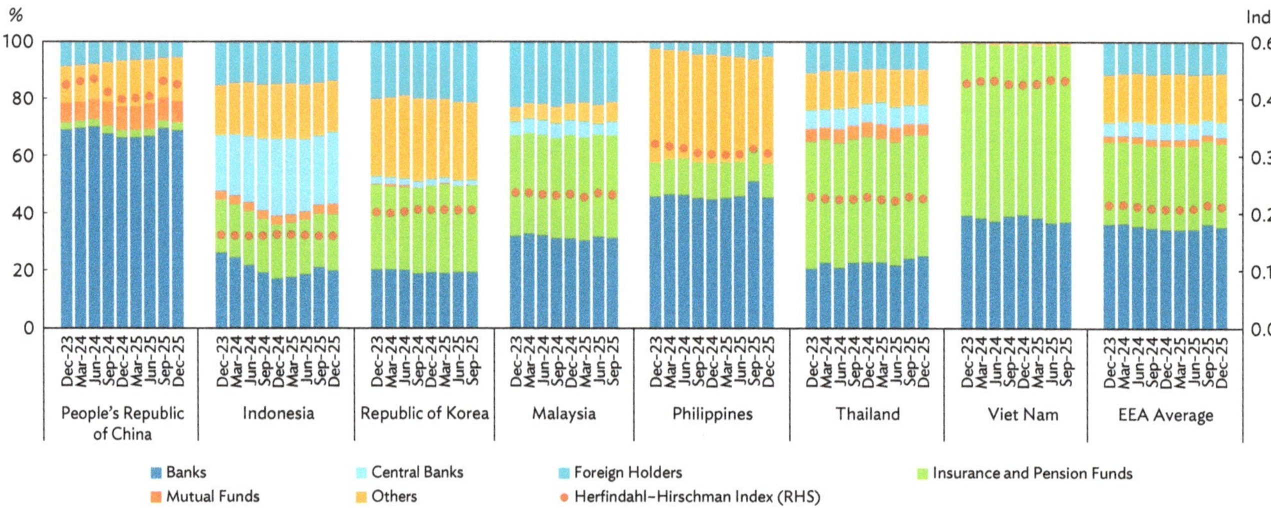


EEA = emerging East Asia, RHS = right-hand side.

Notes:

1. Data for the Republic of Korea, Malaysia, and Viet Nam are up to September 2025.
2. "Others" include government institutions, individuals, securities companies, custodians, private corporations, and all other investors not elsewhere classified.
3. The Herfindahl–Hirschman Index is a commonly accepted measure of market concentration. In this case, the index was used to measure the investor profile diversification of local currency bond markets and is calculated by summing the squared share of each investor group in a bond market. A lower score indicates greater diversity.

Sources: People's Republic of China (CEIC Data Company); Indonesia (Directorate General of Budget Financing and Risk Management, Ministry of Finance); Republic of Korea (Bank of Korea); Malaysia (Bank Negara Malaysia); Philippines (Bureau of the Treasury); Thailand (Bank of Thailand); and Viet Nam (Ministry of Finance).

[6] The Herfindahl–Hirschman Index is a commonly accepted measure of market concentration. The index is used to measure the investor profile diversification of the region's LCY bond markets and is calculated by summing the squared share of each investor group in the bond market. A lower score indicates greater diversity.

## Box 2: When Banks and Insurers Move Together—Why Systemic Risk Lives in the Tails?

### Why Bank–Insurance Linkages Matter More Than Ever?

The global financial system no longer operates in silos.[a] Over the past 2 decades, a significant convergence has occurred: Banks have expanded into insurance and asset management, while insurers have deepened their presence in capital markets through corporate bonds, private equity, derivatives, and structured products (Allen and Jagtiani 2000, Bernardi and Petrella 2015, Foglia and Angelini 2020). As the distinction between bank risk and insurance risk becomes increasingly blurred, regulators and policymakers in Asia and beyond face a critical question:

When shocks hit the financial system, do these institutions absorb risk independently, or do they amplify each other's stress?

### Why Averages Can Be Misleading?

Most empirical measures of financial connectedness, such as correlation or standard vector-autoregression-based spillover indices, focus on mean relationships. These tools are useful, but they implicitly assume that risk transmission is linear and stable across time. However, financial markets are anything but linear. During tranquil periods, banks and insurers may appear loosely connected: Diversification works, shocks are absorbed locally, and institutions retain a degree of independence. But during financial crises, global pandemics, geopolitical conflicts, or sharp monetary tightening, this insulation often disappears.

This box argues that systemic risk between banks and insurers is fundamentally a tail phenomenon. By looking beyond averages and into the extremes of the return distribution, we uncover a striking pattern: Connectedness between banks and insurers intensifies dramatically during periods of market stress and exuberance, while remaining fragmented in normal times.

### What the Data Say: Risk Lives in the Tails?

Using daily stock returns of the world's top 10 banks and top 10 insurance companies from 2016 to 2025, we first examine the basic statistical properties of these returns.[b] The evidence is striking. For instance, average returns are close to zero for both banks and insurers, while volatility is high and heterogeneous across institutions. Return distributions exhibit extreme kurtosis, far exceeding the Gaussian (normal) benchmark, and skewness is generally close to zero, suggesting no obvious dominance of upside or downside risk. In plain language, extreme events occur frequently on both the positive and negative sides of the return distribution, even if the overall distribution does not exhibit a strong skew in one direction.

Visual inspection of the return series reinforces this message (**Figures B2.1** and **B2.2**). Large spikes, both positive and negative, appear in clusters during well-known stress episodes such as the coronavirus disease pandemic and the Russian invasion of Ukraine. These spikes are not isolated outliers; they are a defining feature of the data, occurring in bunches rather than singly. The implication is clear: Systemic risk cannot be understood by looking at averages alone.

### A Quantile Perspective on Connectedness

To capture this tail behavior, we adopt a quantile-based connectedness framework. Instead of estimating spillovers at the mean, we examine how shocks propagate across institutions at different points of the return distribution. In particular, we focus on the lower tail (5th percentile) to represent periods of market stress and distress, the median (50th percentile) for normal market conditions, and the upper tail (95th percentile) to reflect periods of exuberance and risk-taking. This approach allows us to ask whether connectedness behaves differently when markets are calm versus when they are under pressure. The answer is an emphatic "yes" (**Table B2**).

### What Happens to Connectedness Across Market States?

In normal market conditions, total connectedness is moderate and directional, with commercial banks tending to receive shocks, while investment banks (e.g., Bank of America, Goldman Sachs, JP Morgan Chase, and Morgan Stanley) and large insurers (e.g., Allianz SE, Berkshire Hathaway, Chubb, Cigna, Marsh and McLennan, Progressive Corporation, United Health Group) act as transmitters. In this state, diversification offers protection, and risk transmission is selective rather than systemic.

**Normal times: fragmented and directional.** At the median quantile (normal market conditions), total connectedness between banks and insurers is relatively moderate. More importantly, directional patterns emerge: Commercial banks tend to be net receivers of shocks, while market-based

*continued on next page*

## Box 2 *continued*

**Figure B2.1: Daily Bank Returns Illustrating Volatility Clustering and Extreme Movements**

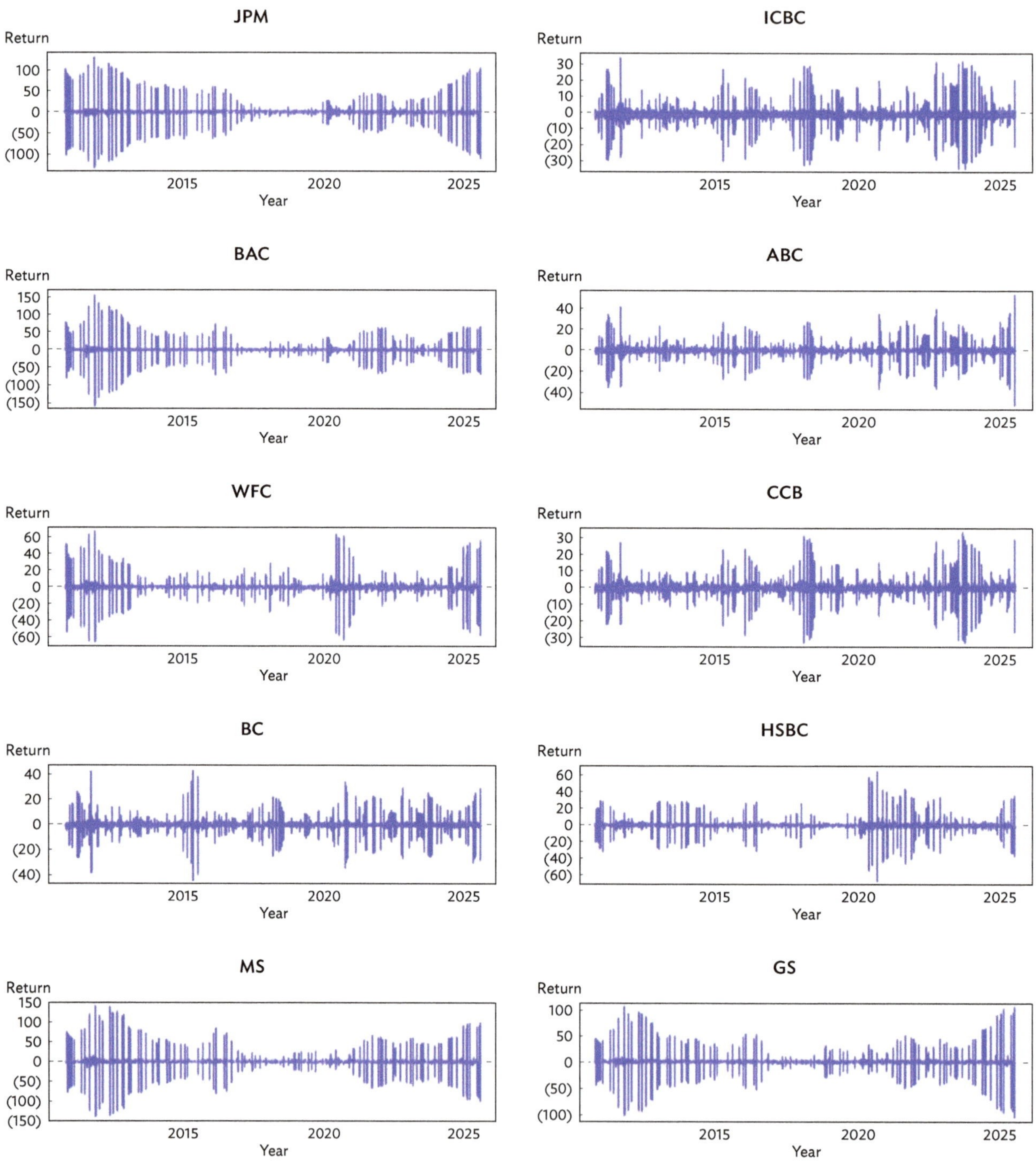


ABC = Agricultural Bank of China, BAC = Bank of America, BC = Bank of China, CCB = China Construction Bank, GS = Goldman Sachs, HSBC = The Hongkong and Shanghai Banking Corporation Limited, ICBC = Industrial and Commercial Bank of China, JPM = JP Morgan Chase, MS = Morgan Stanley, WFC = Wells Fargo.

Source: Yahoo Finance.

*continued on next page*

## Box 2 *continued*

**Figure B2.2: Daily Returns for Insurance Companies Illustrating Volatility Clustering and Extreme Movements**

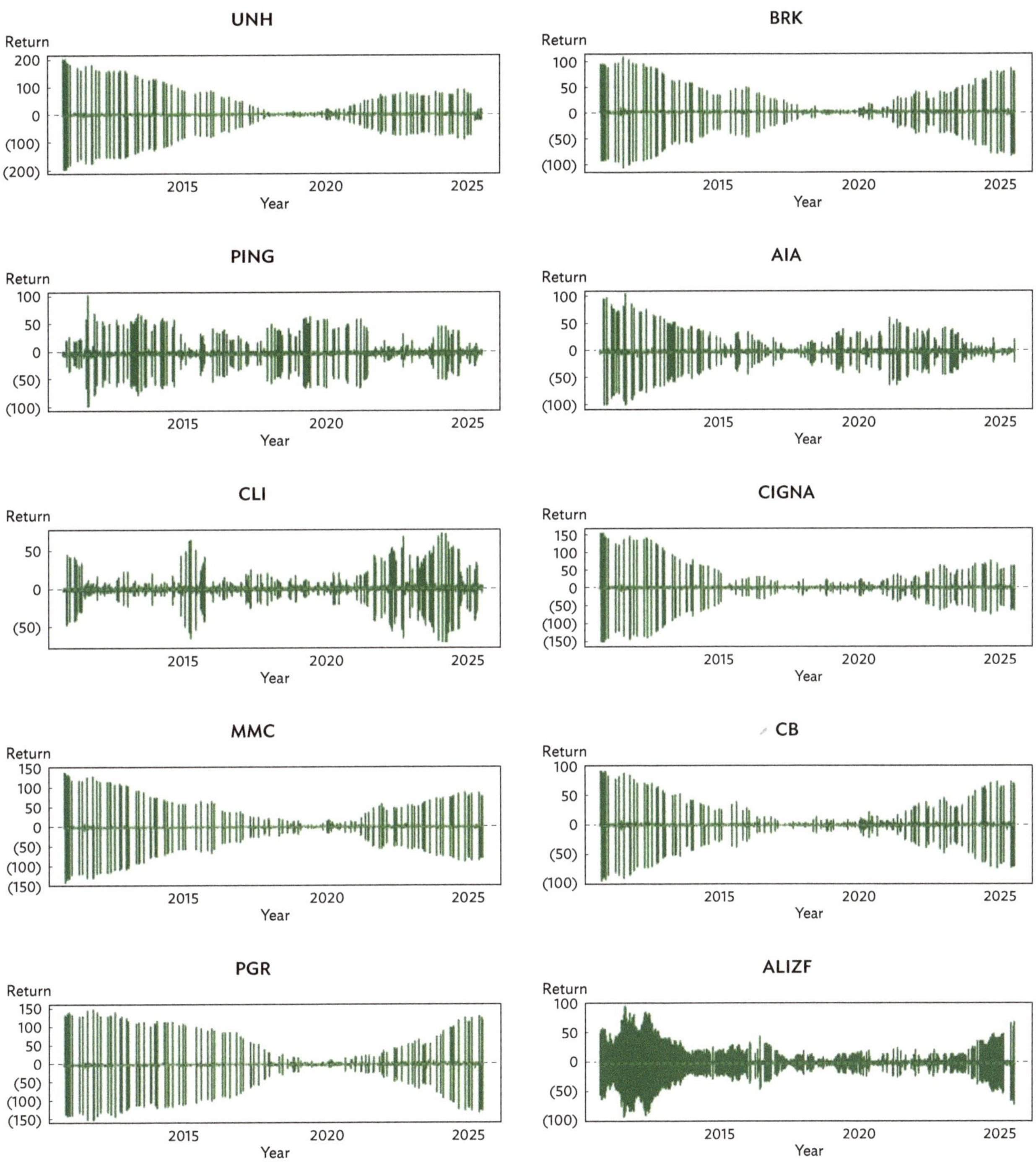


AIA = AIA Group, ALIZF = Allianz SE, BRK = Berkshire Hathaway, CB = Chubb, CIGNA = Cigna, CLI = China Life Insurance, MMC = Marsh and McLennan, PGR = Progressive Corporation, PING = Ping An Insurance, UNH = UnitedHealth Group.

Source: Yahoo Finance.

*continued on next page*

## Box 2 *continued*

**Table B2: Connectedness Between Banks and Insurers**

| | τ = 0.05 | | | | τ = 0.5 | | | | τ = 0.95 | | | |
|---|---|---|---|---|---|---|---|---|---|---|---|---|
| | OWN | FROM | TO | NET | OWN | FROM | TO | NET | OWN | FROM | TO | NET |
| JPM | **4.97** | 95.03 | 92.94 | (2.10) | **13.21** | 86.79 | 102.90 | 16.16 | **5.10** | 94.90 | 94.54 | (0.36) |
| ICBC | **4.80** | 95.20 | 90.23 | (4.97) | **20.80** | 79.20 | 71.46 | (7.74) | **4.76** | 95.24 | 88.84 | (6.40) |
| BAC | **4.94** | 95.06 | 92.79 | (2.27) | **13.10** | 86.90 | 99.15 | 12.26 | **5.19** | 94.81 | 96.21 | 1.40 |
| ABC | **4.89** | 95.11 | 91.68 | (3.43) | **21.62** | 78.38 | 69.36 | (9.02) | **4.93** | 95.07 | 91.38 | (3.68) |
| WFC | **4.90** | 95.10 | 92.25 | (2.85) | **20.22** | 79.78 | 67.52 | (12.26) | **5.30** | 94.70 | 97.62 | 2.92 |
| CCB | **4.82** | 95.18 | 90.77 | (4.41) | **21.28** | 78.72 | 67.13 | (11.59) | **4.71** | 95.29 | 88.54 | (6.75) |
| BC | **4.90** | 95.10 | 91.77 | (3.33) | **21.45** | 78.55 | 70.21 | (8.33) | **5.02** | 94.98 | 92.94 | (2.05) |
| HSBC | **4.92** | 95.08 | 91.36 | (3.72) | **19.89** | 80.11 | 64.72 | (15.39) | **5.41** | 94.59 | 98.81 | 4.22 |
| MS | **5.02** | 94.98 | 94.22 | (0.76) | **12.48** | 87.52 | 101.20 | 13.69 | **5.08** | 94.92 | 94.82 | (0.09) |
| GS | **4.98** | 95.02 | 93.29 | (1.73) | **13.31** | 86.69 | 96.90 | 10.21 | **4.96** | 95.04 | 92.68 | (2.36) |
| UNH | **5.26** | 94.74 | 98.97 | 4.23 | **13.93** | 86.07 | 101.80 | 15.78 | **5.47** | 94.53 | 101.02 | 6.50 |
| BRK | **5.18** | 94.82 | 97.57 | 2.75 | **13.15** | 86.85 | 103.70 | 16.92 | **5.01** | 94.99 | 95.10 | 0.11 |
| PING | **5.06** | 94.94 | 93.80 | (1.15) | **30.05** | 69.95 | 56.01 | (13.94) | **5.10** | 94.90 | 95.13 | 0.23 |
| AIA | **5.24** | 94.76 | 97.35 | 2.59 | **29.18** | 70.82 | 58.61 | (12.21) | **5.26** | 94.74 | 98.15 | 3.40 |
| CLI | **5.04** | 94.96 | 95.17 | 0.21 | **26.69** | 73.31 | 56.75 | (16.56) | **5.11** | 94.89 | 95.87 | 0.98 |
| CIGNA | **5.09** | 94.91 | 96.03 | 1.12 | **14.34** | 85.66 | 95.45 | 9.79 | **4.91** | 95.09 | 92.69 | (2.40) |
| MMC | **5.53** | 94.47 | 104.10 | 9.68 | **12.19** | 87.81 | 108.40 | 20.61 | **5.33** | 94.67 | 100.08 | 5.40 |
| CB | **5.14** | 94.86 | 97.33 | 2.47 | **14.86** | 85.14 | 94.58 | 9.44 | **4.88** | 95.12 | 92.44 | (2.68) |
| PGR | **5.58** | 94.42 | 104.00 | 9.63 | **13.90** | 86.10 | 103.90 | 17.79 | **5.22** | 94.78 | 97.93 | 3.16 |
| ALIZF | **4.98** | 95.02 | 93.05 | (1.97) | **43.43** | 56.57 | 20.97 | (35.60) | **4.97** | 95.03 | 93.48 | (1.55) |
| **TCI** | | **94.94** | | | | | **80.55** | | | | **94.91** | |

( ) = negative, ABC = Agricultural Bank of China, AIA = AIA Group, ALIZF = Allianz SE, BAC = Bank of China, BOA = Bank of America, BRK = Berkshire Hathaway, CB = Chubb, CCB = China Construction Bank, CLI=China Life Insurance, CIGNA = Cigna, GS = Goldman Sachs, HSBC = The Hongkong and Shanghai Banking Corporation Limited, ICBC = Industrial and Commercial Bank of China, JPM = JP Morgan Chase, MMC = Marsh and McLennan, MS = Morgan Stanley, PING = Ping An Insurance, PGR = Progressive Corporation, TCI = Total Connectedness Index, UNH = United Health Group, WFC = Wells Fargo.

Source: Yahoo Finance.

institutions, including investment banks and large insurers, often act as net transmitters. In other words, spillovers have a clear direction and structure. In these conditions, diversification still offers some protection, and risk transmission remains selective rather than systemic.

**Stress and exuberance: synchronized and overwhelming.** In extreme market conditions, the picture changes dramatically: At both the lower and upper quantiles, the Total Connectedness Index jumps to nearly 100%. In these states, institutions explain almost all of each other's forecast error variance. As a result, own risk becomes negligible and any directionality collapses into system-wide synchronization. In simple terms, when markets enter extreme conditions, banks and insurers stop behaving as separate entities and instead move as a tightly coupled network. Notably, this result holds for both downturns and booms, indicating that exuberant markets can be just as systemically connected as distressed ones.

### Asymmetry Across States, Not Just Positive or Negative Shocks

A key insight from the analysis is that the asymmetry lies not only between negative (downside) and positive (upside) shocks, but more fundamentally between normal and extreme market states. During normal times (median quantile), connectedness across institutions is moderate but more volatile, and risk transmission follows a directional pattern with identifiable transmitters and receivers.
In contrast, during extreme states, whether driven by distress (5th percentile) or exuberance (95th percentile),

*continued on next page*

**Box 2** *continued*

connectedness becomes extremely high and persistent, with institutions moving in near lockstep and the usual distinctions between shock transmitters and receivers disappearing. This state-dependent asymmetry suggests that systemic risk is not constant but conditional: It flares up precisely when the system becomes most vulnerable.

### Why Banks and Insurers Amplify Each Other?

These findings help explain why bank–insurance linkages have become a central concern for regulators. Modern insurers are deeply exposed to financial markets through large investment portfolios, substantial corporate bond holdings, and extensive use of derivatives and reinsurance networks. Similarly, banks have increasingly ventured beyond traditional lending, relying more on noninterest income and market-based activities. When asset prices move sharply, both sectors are affected simultaneously, creating feedback loops that amplify shocks. Our results suggest that such cross-sector spillovers are not a sideshow—they are a core channel of systemic risk, particularly under extreme market conditions.

### Policy Implications for Central Banks and Supervisors

The implications for policymakers in member economies of Southeast Asian Central Banks and beyond are significant. Monitoring averages is not enough. Traditional indicators may underestimate systemic risk precisely when it is building up; tail-sensitive tools are essential for early warning systems. Stress tests should be asymmetric. Stress testing frameworks should explicitly account for nonlinear spillovers and state-dependent amplification, rather than assuming proportional responses.

Cross-sector coordination is critical. Banking and insurance supervision cannot remain siloed. During extreme market conditions, risks propagate seamlessly across sectors. Diversification benefits vanish in crises. Portfolio diversification across banks and insurers may appear effective in calm periods, but these benefits collapse when connectedness spikes in the tails.

### Conclusion

Asian financial systems are increasingly integrated into global capital markets. As banks and insurers in the region expand their operations across borders, the potential for cross-border and cross-sector contagion grows. Understanding when and how connectedness intensifies can help regional authorities design better macroprudential buffers, coordinate responses across regulatory agencies, and anticipate systemic vulnerabilities before they materialize.

The key message from this research is simple but powerful: Systemic risk between banks and insurers is not constant; it emerges in the tails. By shifting our focus from averages to extremes, we gain a clearer picture of how financial shocks propagate and why crises feel so overwhelming when they occur. For policymakers, the lesson is equally clear: To safeguard financial stability, we must look where the risk actually lives, not at the center but at the edges of the distribution.

### References

Allen, L., and J. Jagtiani. 2000. The Risk Effects of Combining Banking, Securities, and Insurance Activities. *Journal of Economics and Business* 52 (6). pp. 485–497. https://doi.org/10.1016/s0148-6195(00)00033-3.

Bernardi, M., G. Gayraud, and L. Petrella. 2015. Bayesian Tail Risk Interdependence Using Quantile Regression. *Bayesian Analysis* 10. pp. 553–603. https://doi.org/10.1214/14-ba911.

Foglia, M., and E. Angelini. 2020. From Me To You: Measuring Connectedness between Eurozone Financial Institutions. *Research in International Business and Finance* 54 (C). https://doi.org/10.1016/j.ribaf.2020.101238.

This box was written by Nur Ain Shahrier (senior economist) at the South East Asian Central Banks Centre (SEACEN), and by Noureddine Benlagha (professor), Fahad Shafiq (master's student in finance), and Rashid Hassan Al-Derham (master's student in finance) from the Department of Finance and Economics, College of Business and Economics, Qatar University, Doha, Qatar.

[a] This article draws on the working paper, When Banks and Insurers Move Together: Why Systemic Risk Lives in the Tails?, which is available at https://lnkd.in/ggTAUzRG.

[b] The top 10 global banks in our sample, listed alphabetically, are Agricultural Bank of China (ABC), Bank of America (BAC), Bank of China (BC), China Construction Bank (939 HK), Goldman Sachs (GS), HSBC, Industrial and Commercial Bank of China (ICBC), JP Morgan Chase (JPM), Morgan Stanley (MS), and Wells Fargo (WFC). The top 10 global insurance companies are AIA Group (1299 HK), Allianz SE (ALIZF), Berkshire Hathaway (BRK.B), Chubb (CB), Cigna (CI), China Life Insurance (2628 HK), Marsh & McLennan (MMC), Ping An Insurance (2318 HK), Progressive Corporation (PGR), and UnitedHealth Group (UNH).

# Section 2. Local Currency Bond Issuance

**Emerging East Asian LCY bond issuance fell in Q4 2025 as both government and corporate borrowing declined.** Total LCY bond issuance contracted 11.1% q-o-q in Q4 2025 to USD2.9 trillion (**Figure 3A**). For full-year 2025, however, total issuance rose 12.7% year-on-year to USD12.0 trillion from USD10.7 trillion in 2024 on accommodative monetary stances.

- Issuance of government bonds contracted 22.0% q-o-q in Q4 2025, following 1.1% q-o-q growth in Q3 2025, as a majority of governments in the region had already fulfilled most of their annual borrowing plans in previous quarters. Government bond issuance in the PRC, which comprised 86.6% of the region's government issuance total in Q4 2025, contracted 22.6% q-o-q, driven by reduced issuance of local government bonds and policy bank bonds (**Figure 3B**). Issuance in the PRC fell as local governments had fulfilled most of their annual quotas in prior quarters and as policy banks had previously accelerated bond issuance ahead of the reimposition of the value added tax on interest income in August. Issuance in the Republic of Korea and ASEAN member economies also decreased in Q4 2025, falling 30.4% q-o-q and 17.8% q-o-q, respectively, reflecting most governments' front-loading issuance policies. On the other hand, issuance in Hong Kong, China rose almost ninefold in Q4 2025, in line with the planned auction schedule for the year and amid the outsized issuance of Silver Bonds in October (HKD55.0 billion).[7]
- Corporate bond sales fell 3.3% q-o-q in Q4 2025 to USD1.1 trillion, a reversal from the 5.1% q-o-q growth in Q3 2025, led by contractions in the PRC and ASEAN member economies. Issuance of corporate bonds in the PRC fell 5.4% q-o-q amid continued weak borrowing demand that was driven by economic uncertainty. Corporate bond issuance in ASEAN decreased 9.3% q-o-q in Q4 2025 as bond yields rose in most member economies, largely tracking the upward movement of yields in advanced economies as well as market-specific factors. In the Republic of Korea, corporate bond issuance rose 21.0% q-o-q as banks ramped up issuance to secure liquidity amid an outflow of bank deposits in Q4 2025. Investors in the Republic of Korea shifted their funds from low-yield bank instruments to the domestic stock market, which witnessed significant gains during the year.
- Central bank bond issuance in emerging East Asia decreased 0.3% q-o-q in Q4 2025, led by reduced issuance from most ASEAN central banks.

**Figure 3: Local Currency Bond Issuance in Select Emerging East Asian Markets**

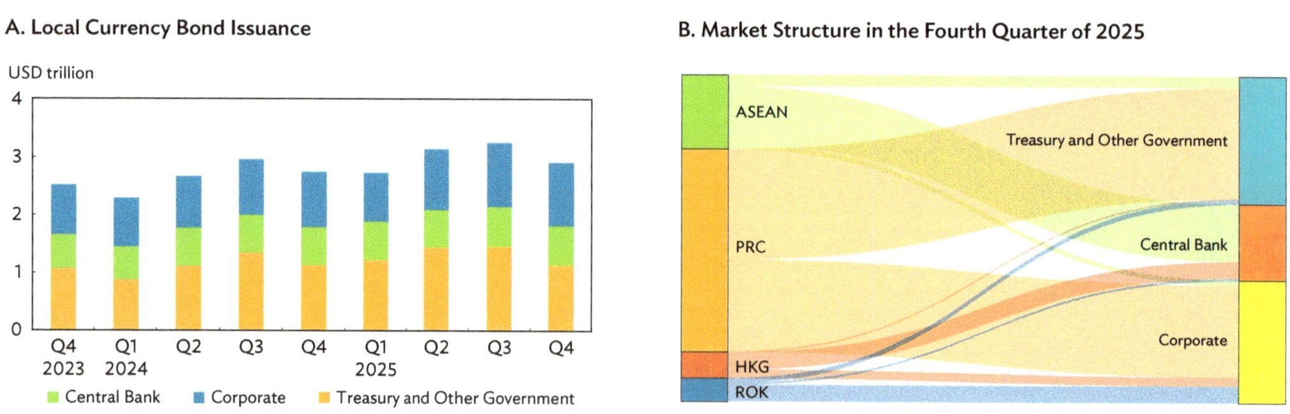


ASEAN = Association of Southeast Asian Nations; PRC = People's Republic of China; HKG = Hong Kong, China; ROK = Republic of Korea; Q1 = first quarter; Q2 = second quarter; Q3 = third quarter; Q4 = fourth quarter; USD = United States dollar.

Notes:
1. ASEAN data include the markets of Indonesia, Malaysia, the Philippines, Singapore, Thailand, and Viet Nam.
2. Figures were computed based on 31 December 2025 currency exchange rates and do not include currency effects.

Source: *AsianBondsOnline* calculations based on various local market sources.

[7] Silver Bonds are 3-year government bonds specifically offered and catered to senior citizens in Hong Kong, China.

**The size-weighted average maturity of Treasury bond issuances in emerging East Asia declined to 8.1 years in Q4 2025 from 11.4 years in Q3 2025 on increased short-term issuances.** The share of Treasury bond issuances with a maturity of 5 years or less rose to 50.5% in Q4 2025 from 46.4% in the previous quarter (**Figure 4A**). In Hong Kong, China, the share of Treasury bond issuances with a maturity of more than 5 years (medium- to long-term bonds) plunged to 2.5% in Q4 2025 from 43.5% in Q3 2025, as the HKD55.0 billion worth of 3-year Silver Bonds sold by the government in October accounted for about 90% of quarterly issuance (**Figure 4B**). In the PRC, during the same period, the share of medium- to long-term Treasury bond issuances declined to 47.5% from 53.0% due to the reduced issuance of ultra-long-term special Treasury bonds, with the last tranche issued in October. In the Republic of Korea, the share of medium- to long-term bond issuances fell to 43.2% from 48.9%, driven by increased issuance of 2–5 year bonds. Medium- to long-term Treasury bond issuances comprised 70.9% of total Treasury bond issuance in ASEAN in Q4 2025, up from 63.0% in the previous quarter, lengthening the size-weighted average maturity to 12.7 years from 11.6 years. Viet Nam and Malaysia had the highest percentages of medium- to long-term bond issuances in Q4 2025 at 86.5% and 80.4%, respectively. Singapore registered the longest size-weighted average maturity in the region at 16.3 years.

**Figure 4: Maturity Structure of Local Currency Treasury Bond Issuance in Emerging East Asian Markets**

**A. Maturity Structure by Quarter** **B. Maturity Structure by Market**

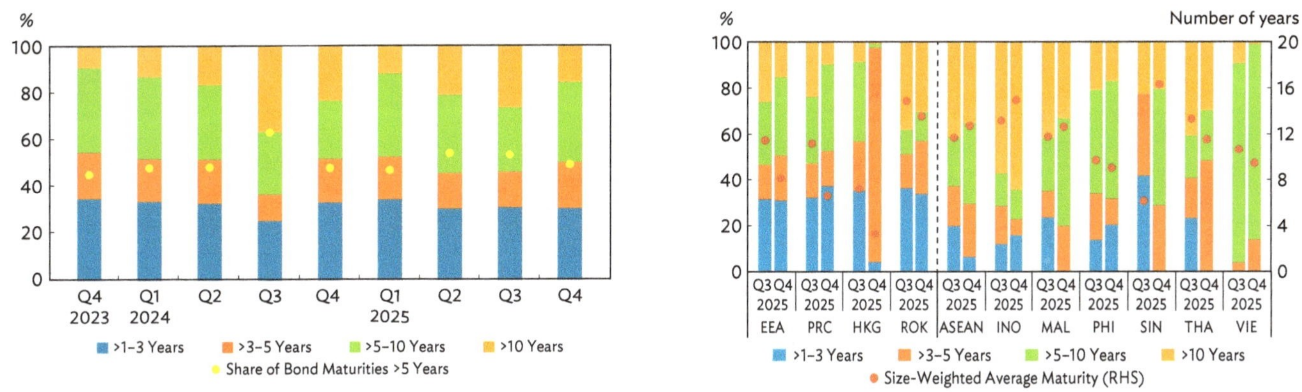


ASEAN = Association of Southeast Asian Nations; PRC = People's Republic of China; EEA = emerging East Asia; HKG = Hong Kong, China; INO = Indonesia; ROK = Republic of Korea; MAL = Malaysia; PHI = Philippines; Q1 = first quarter; Q2 = second quarter; Q3 = third quarter; Q4 = fourth quarter; RHS = right-hand side; SIN = Singapore; THA = Thailand; VIE = Viet Nam.

Notes:

1. Figures were computed based on 31 December 2025 currency exchange rates and do not include currency effects.
2. Treasury bonds are local-currency-denominated, fixed-income securities issued by a government with maturities longer than 1 year.
3. Emerging East Asia is defined to include member states of the Association of Southeast Asian Nations plus the People's Republic of China; Hong Kong, China; and the Republic of Korea.

Source: *AsianBondsOnline* calculations based on various local market sources.

## Section 3: Intra-Regional Bond Issuance

**Emerging East Asia's intra-regional bond issuance increased 18.7% q-o-q in Q4 2025, supported by improved financial conditions.**[8] The region's intra-regional debt sales rose to USD17.0 billion from the previous quarter's USD14.3 billion, while full-year 2025 issuance tallied USD52.1 billion, up 20.0% from USD43.4 billion in 2024 (**Figure 5A**). Growth in Q4 2025 was bolstered by increased debt sales in Hong Kong, China (USD13.0 billion) and the Republic of Korea (USD1.1 billion), as well as by the return of Malaysia (USD0.9 billion), Indonesia (USD0.9 billion), Thailand (USD0.1 billion), and Viet Nam (USD0.02 billion) to the intra-regional bond market.

- Emerging East Asia's intra-regional bond market was dominated by issuers from Hong Kong, China, which accounted for 76.6% of the intra-regional total (**Figure 5B**). The Chinese yuan remained the primary currency of choice among intra-regional bond issuers in Q4 2025, accounting for 84.8% of the regional total. HKD-

**Figure 5: Intra-Regional Bond Issuance in Emerging East Asian Markets**

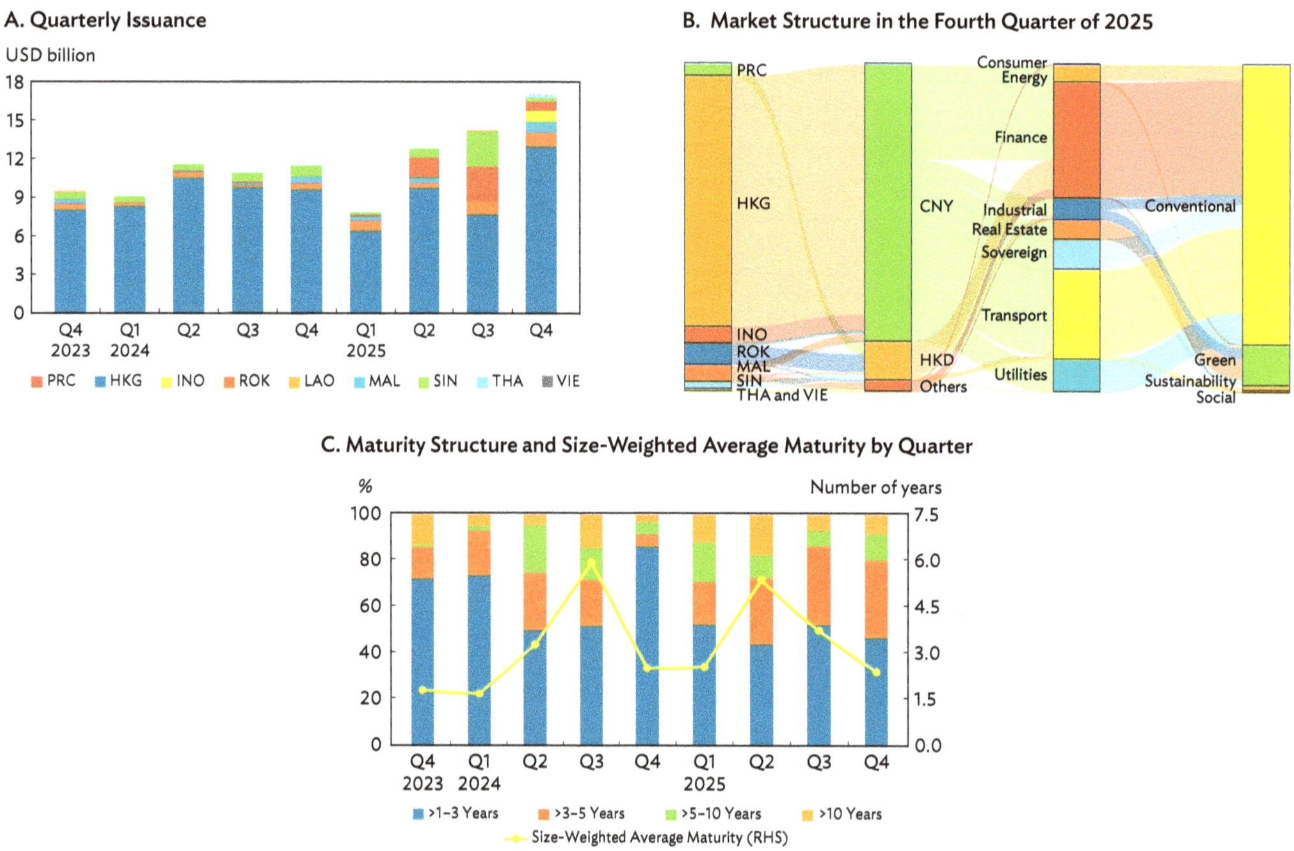


PRC = People's Republic of China; CNY = Chinese yuan; HKD = Hong Kong dollar; HKG = Hong Kong, China; INO = Indonesia; ROK = Republic of Korea; LAO = Lao People's Democratic Republic; MAL = Malaysia; Q1 = first quarter; Q2 = second quarter; Q3 = third quarter; Q4 = fourth quarter; RHS = right-hand side; SIN = Singapore; THA = Thailand; USD = United States dollar; VIE = Viet Nam.

Notes:

1. Emerging East Asia is defined to include member states of the Association of Southeast Asian Nations plus the People's Republic of China; Hong Kong, China; and the Republic of Korea.
2. Intra-regional bond issuance is defined as emerging East Asian bond issuance denominated in a regional currency excluding the issuer's home currency.
3. Figures were computed based on 31 December 2025 currency exchange rates and do not include currency effects.
4. Data are based on the domicile where the company's senior management is located.
5. Other currencies include Korean won and Singapore dollar.

Source: *AsianBondsOnline* calculations based on Bloomberg LP data.

[8] Intra-regional bond issuance is defined as emerging East Asian bond issuance denominated in a regional currency excluding the issuer's home currency.

denominated bonds accounted for 11.8%, down from 25.3% in Q3 2025.

- Corporate bonds accounted for 90.9% of total emerging East Asian intra-regional bond issuance in Q4 2025, largely driven by the financial (39.0%) and transportation (30.3%) sectors. Hong Kong, China's China Merchants Group was the region's leading intra-regional issuer, with aggregate issuance of CNY28.0 billion, representing 23.6% of the total in Q4 2025.
- Sustainable bond issuance in the region's intra-regional bond market increased to USD2.5 billion in Q4 2025 from USD1.4 billion in the previous quarter. There were six green bond issuances from Hong Kong, China, totaling CNY14.7 billion. Korea Expressway Corporation also issued sustainability bonds worth HKD2.0 billion. Thailand returned to the intra-regional bond market for the first time since March 2023 via Muangthai Capital's dual-tranche social bonds worth SGD129.0 million. Despite this growth, the region's intra-regional bond market remained dominated by conventional instruments, which accounted for 85.6% of total intra-regional bond issuance during Q4 2025.
- Most intra-regional bond issuances in Q4 2025 were concentrated in short- to medium-term maturities, lowering the size-weighted average maturity to 2.4 years from 3.7 years in Q3 2025. Issuances with maturities of 5 years or less accounted for 80.1% of the total in Q4 2025, with issuance volume heavily skewed toward shorter tenors (**Figure 5C**).

## Section 4. G3 Currency Bond Issuance

**Emerging East Asian G3 currency bond issuance fell 10.8% q-o-q to USD96.2 billion in Q4 2025 from a high base in the previous quarter, when issuance surged to USD107.8 billion.**[9] The reversal from the previous quarter's 45.5% q-o-q growth in the region's G3 currency bond issuance was due to reduced corporate issuance (**Figure 6A**). Weaker issuance in Q4 2025 capped otherwise robust annual issuance of G3-denominated bonds in 2025, which rose 41.7% year-on-year to USD351.4 billion as US interest rates declined.

- Corporate issuances comprised 76.1% of G3-denominated bond issuances in emerging East Asia in Q4 2025, with only 23.9% of the total issued by public sector entities. G3-denominated corporate bond sales were dominated by the real estate (33.2%), financial (28.6%), and industrial (12.2%) sectors. The real estate sector's G3 bond issuance during the quarter was buoyed by increased issuance from the PRC.
- The PRC led emerging East Asia's G3 issuance in Q4 2025 with USD61.8 billion, accounting for 64.2% of the regional total on a 10.3% q-o-q increase. The increase was buoyed by real estate companies' debt-restructuring programs. Country Garden and Sunac China issued USD-denominated bonds worth an aggregate USD22.6 billion, which comprised 23.5% of the regional quarterly total. The Government of the PRC sold EUR- and USD-denominated issuances worth USD8.7 billion, reinforcing the PRC's offshore market presence.[10]
- G3 bond issuance from ASEAN economies tallied USD18.6 billion in Q4 2025, contracting 24.1% q-o-q and accounting for 19.3% of the region's quarterly total (**Figure 6B**). G3-denominated issuance from ASEAN economies fell on reduced corporate issuance, which declined 34.1% q-o-q. Several ASEAN economies saw reduced G3 bond issuance, including the Philippines (–65.3% q-o-q), Singapore (–55.0% q-o-q), Thailand (–24.1% q-o-q), and Indonesia (–8.1% q-o-q). The Lao People's Democratic Republic issued USD0.3 billion worth of notes for government refinancing, its first offshore foreign currency bond issuance since 2019.
- The share of EUR-denominated bonds in the region's total G3 issuance increased in Q4 2025 to 11.8% from 9.3% in the previous quarter as borrowing costs for EUR-denominated assets decreased and investors sought portfolio diversification.[11]
- Over half (59.4%) of G3 issuances in Q4 2025 carried a maturity of 5 years or less, down slightly from 59.8% in Q3 2025 (**Figure 6C**). The size-weighted average maturity of regional G3 bond issuance fell to 5.0 years in Q4 2025 from 5.6 years in the previous quarter.

---

[9] G3 currency bonds are bonds denominated in either euros, Japanese yen, or United States dollars.

[10] Zxouxiang, Z., and J. Xueqing. 2025. Nation's Euro Bond Sale Shows Investors' Confidence. *China Daily*. 21 November.

[11] *Business Times*. 2025. US Loses Financing Edge as Asia Borrows in Euros. 7 December.

**Figure 6: G3 Currency Bond Issuance in Emerging East Asian Markets**

**A. Monthly Bond Issuance by Currency**

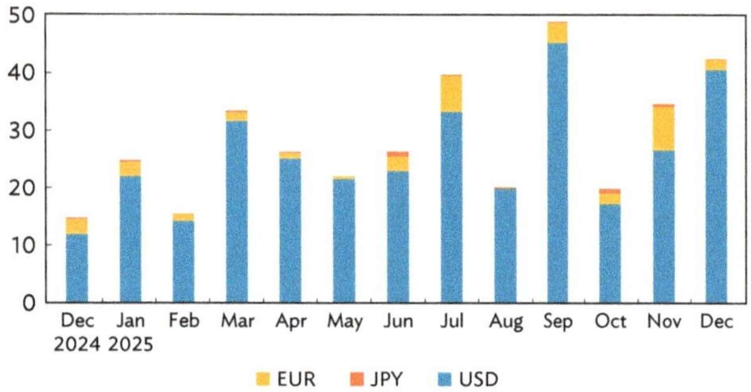


**B. Market Shares in the Fourth Quarter of 2025**

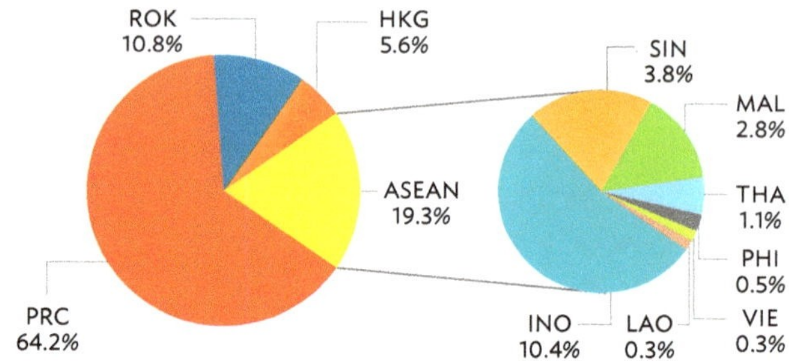


**C. Maturity Structure and Size-Weighted Average Maturity by Subgroup**

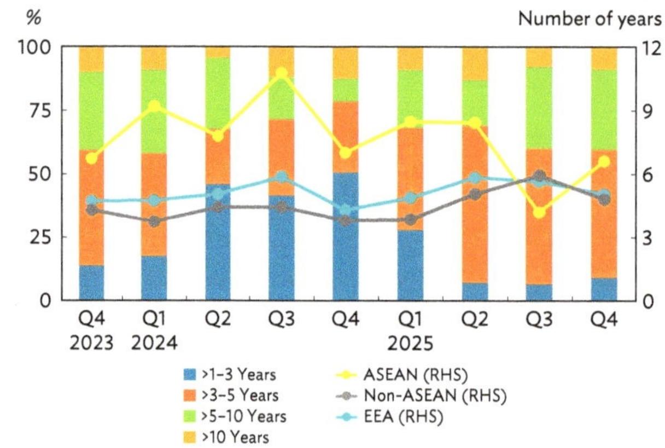


ASEAN = Association of Southeast Asian Nations; PRC = People's Republic of China; EEA = emerging East Asia; EUR = euro; HKG = Hong Kong, China; INO = Indonesia; JPY = Japanese yen; ROK = Republic of Korea; LAO = Lao People's Democratic Republic; MAL = Malaysia; PHI = Philippines; Q1 = first quarter; Q2 = second quarter; Q3 = third quarter; Q4 = fourth quarter; RHS = right-hand side; SIN = Singapore; THA = Thailand; USD = United States dollar; VIE = Viet Nam.

Notes:

1. Emerging East Asia is defined to include the member states of ASEAN plus the People's Republic of China; Hong Kong, China; and the Republic of Korea. ASEAN data include the markets of Indonesia, Malaysia, the Philippines, Singapore, Thailand, and Viet Nam.
2. G3 currency bonds are denominated in either euros, Japanese yen, or United States dollars.
3. Figures were computed based on 31 December 2025 currency exchange rates and do not include currency effects.

Source: *AsianBondsOnline* calculations based on Bloomberg LP data.

# Section 5. Liquidity of LCY Bond Markets

**Emerging East Asian LCY bond markets witnessed improved liquidity in 2025, buoyed by favorable financial conditions over monetary policy easing and sound economic fundamentals across the region.**[12] Turnover ratios and average trading volumes for both LCY government and corporate bonds rose in 2025, while bid–ask spreads witnessed marginal declines in most regional markets.

## Government Bond Markets

**Bid–ask spreads for LCY government bonds narrowed in most regional markets in 2025 amid monetary policy easing.** The region's average bid–ask spread for on-the-run LCY government bonds remained at 5.7 basis points (bps), the same as in 2024, as the widening of spreads in the Philippines and Viet Nam offset narrowing in most regional markets (**Figure 7A**). The bid–ask spread widened the most in Viet Nam, by 3 bps, amid tightened financial conditions and decreased risk appetite over a rapid credit expansion aimed to support the government's economic growth targets. In the Philippines, the slight widening of the bid–ask spread, by 0.5 bps, was largely due to the reduced supply of bonds in Q4 2025 as the government scaled back issuance following outsized issuances of 10-year bonds and retail Treasury bonds in earlier quarters. Bid–ask spreads for off-the-run LCY government bonds narrowed in all regional economies in 2025 except the PRC, the Philippines, and Viet Nam (**Figure 7B**). The uptick in bid–ask spreads in these three markets pushed up the regional average to 6.6 bps in 2025 from 6.3 bps a year earlier. The bid–ask spread for off-the-run government bonds widened to 2.7 bps from 2.4 bps in the PRC, partly driven by a decline in trading volume caused by the People's Bank of China's bond-buying pause in January–October 2025, which reduced bond trading activity and market liquidity.

**Figure 7: Average Bid–Ask Spreads for Local Currency Government Bonds**

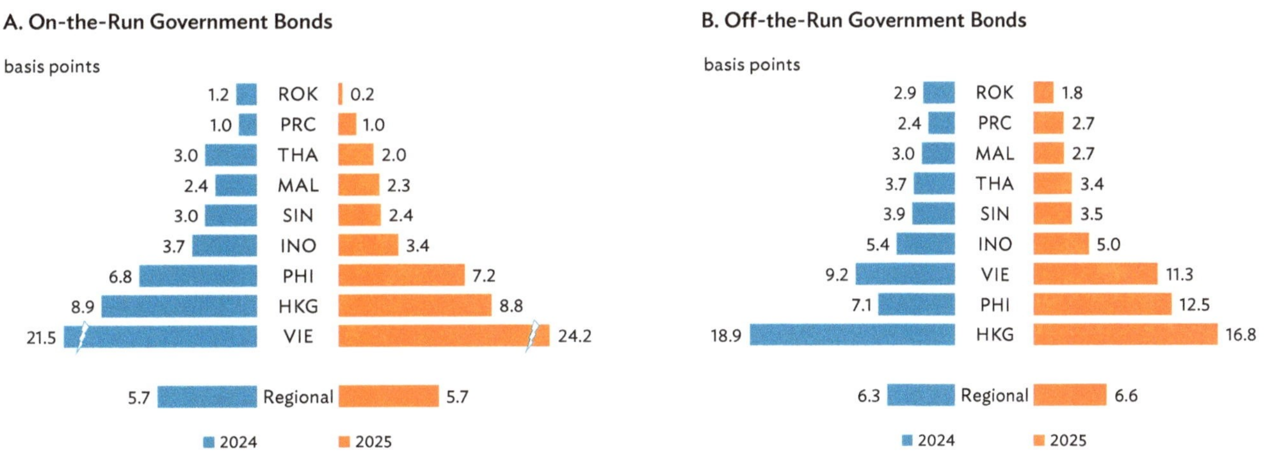


PRC = People's Republic of China; HKG = Hong Kong, China; INO = Indonesia; ROK = Republic of Korea; MAL = Malaysia; PHI = Philippines; SIN = Singapore; THA = Thailand; VIE = Viet Nam.

Note: The regional bid–ask spread refers to the average spread of the nine markets of emerging East Asia.

Source: *AsianBondsOnline* calculations based on Bloomberg LP data.

12 Emerging East Asia is defined to include member states of the Association of Southeast Asian Nations plus the People's Republic of China; Hong Kong, China; and the Republic of Korea.

**Turnover ratios in most government bond markets in the region increased in 2025, supported by monetary policy easing.** Higher turnover ratios were witnessed in six out of nine regional bond markets in 2025, supported by monetary policy easing from several regional central banks. Turnover ratios were higher in the second and third quarters of 2025, when most rate cuts were conducted (**Figure 8A**). Most markets registered higher average trading volumes in 2025 compared to 2024 (**Figure 8B**). However, the PRC and Hong Kong, China witnessed less trading activity in 2025 than in the prior year, resulting in the regional average turnover ratio (0.45) not changing between 2024 and 2025. The reduced trading volumes in the PRC and Hong Kong, China were partly driven by investors return chasing by shifting from bonds to equities over optimism in the AI and technology sectors. In the PRC, the decline in the turnover ratio in 2025 was partly driven by the central bank halting government bond purchases from January to October 2025.

**Figure 8: Local Currency Government Bond Turnover Ratios and Trading Volumes in Emerging East Asian Markets**

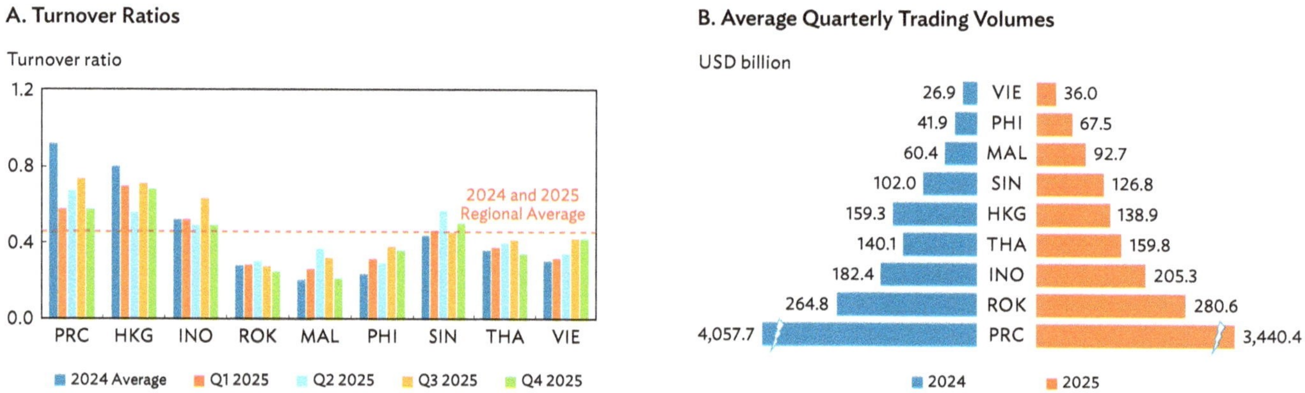


PRC = People's Republic of China; HKG = Hong Kong, China; INO = Indonesia; ROK = Republic of Korea; MAL = Malaysia; PHI = Philippines; Q1 = first quarter; Q2 = second quarter; Q3 = third quarter; Q4 = fourth quarter; SIN = Singapore; THA = Thailand; VIE = Viet Nam.

Notes:

1. Turnover ratios are calculated as the local currency trading volume (sales amount only) divided by the average local currency value of outstanding bonds during each 3-month period.
2. For 2024 average turnover ratios, figures are based on the simple average of quarterly turnover ratios for each market.
3. For Viet Nam, the Q4 2025 turnover ratio was carried over from Q3 2025.
4. For quarterly average trading volumes, figures are based on the simple average of quarterly trading volumes for each market.

Sources: *AsianBondsOnline* calculations based on various local market sources.

## Corporate Bond Markets

**Liquidity in regional corporate bond markets remained largely stable in 2025, supported by continued monetary easing.** The region's overall corporate bid–ask spread narrowed slightly to 17.1 bps in 2025 from 17.4 bps in 2024 (**Figure 9**). Corporate bid–ask spreads fell the most in Indonesia, by 1.8 s, over continued monetary policy easing by Bank Indonesia, particularly in Q3 2025. In Singapore, bid–ask spreads declined 1.6 bps from 2024 to 2025 amid easing adjustments to the Singapore dollar nominal effective exchange rate and a recovery in corporate bond demand over stronger-than-expected economic growth. Singapore's GDP expanded 5.0% on an annual basis in 2025. While liquidity remained stable in the Philippines, it had the widest bid–ask spreads in both 2024 and 2025, driven by a relatively shallow corporate bond market with few active issuers.

**Figure 9: Average Bid–Ask Spreads for Local Currency Corporate Bonds**

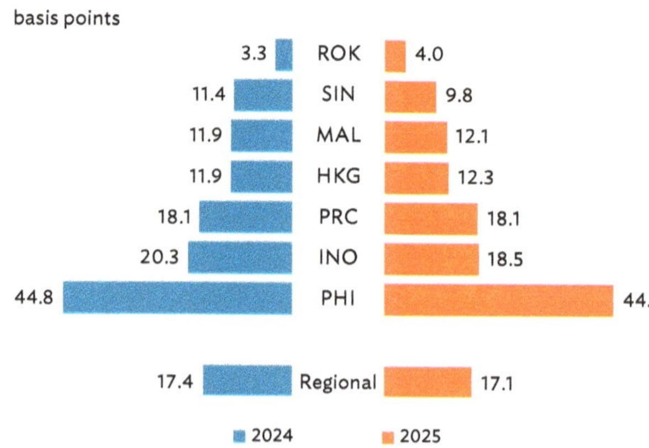


PRC = People's Republic of China; HKG = Hong Kong, China; INO = Indonesia; ROK = Republic of Korea; MAL = Malaysia; PHI = Philippines; SIN = Singapore.

Note: The regional bid–ask spread refers to the average spread of the seven markets of emerging East Asia for which where data are available.

Source: *AsianBondsOnline* calculations based on Bloomberg LP data.

**The region's average corporate bond turnover ratio slightly improved in 2025.** The regional turnover ratio for corporate bonds averaged 0.16 in 2025, up from 0.12 in 2024. While most emerging East Asian markets saw an increase in their respective trading volumes during the review period, corporate bond trading volumes were still much lower than those for government bonds across the region—with the average turnover ratio being less than one-third that for government bonds (**Figure 10A**). Indonesia saw a notable improvement in its corporate bond turnover ratio in the first 3 quarters of 2025, as declining interest rates boosted investor appetite amid a significant amount of maturities and refinancing. The corporate bond turnover ratio in the Philippines was stable during the review period, remaining the lowest in the region as most investors in this market tend to buy and hold corporate bonds until maturity. The Philippines also had the lowest annual trading volume in the region in 2025 at only USD0.6 billion (**Figure 10B**).

**Figure 10: Local Currency Corporate Bond Turnover Ratios and Trading Volumes in Emerging East Asian Markets**

**A. Turnover Ratios** **B. Trading Volumes**

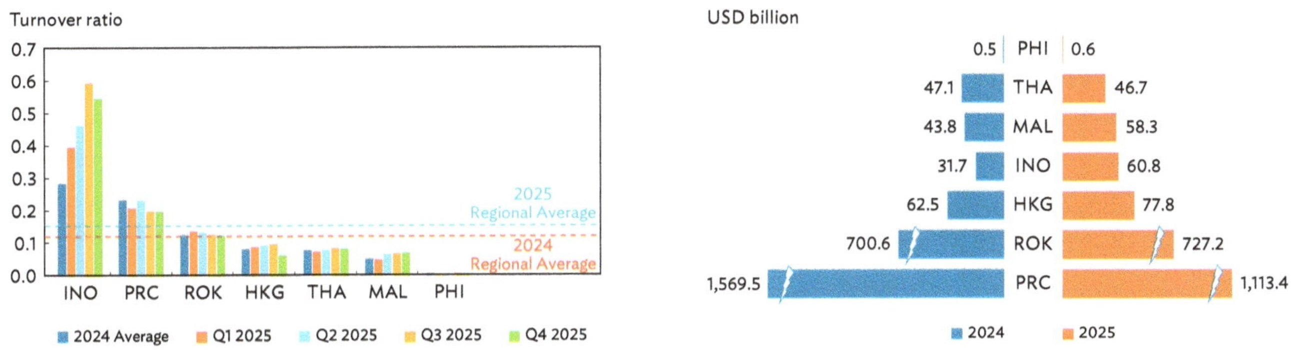


PRC = People's Republic of China; HKG = Hong Kong, China; INO = Indonesia; ROK = Republic of Korea; MAL = Malaysia; PHI = Philippines; Q1 = first quarter; Q2 = second quarter; Q3 = third quarter; Q4 = fourth quarter; THA = Thailand; USD = United States dollar.

Notes:

1. Turnover ratios are calculated as the local currency trading volume (sales amount only) divided by the average local currency value of outstanding bonds during each 3-month period.
2. For 2024 and 2025 averages, figures are based on a simple average of the quarterly turnover ratios for each market.

Sources: *AsianBondsOnline* calculations based on various local market sources.

# Appendix

## Table A1: Size and Composition of Select Emerging East Asian Local Currency Bond Markets

| | Q4 2024 | | Q3 2025 | | Q4 2025 | | | Growth Rate (%) Q4 2025 | |
|---|---|---|---|---|---|---|---|---|---|
| | Amount (USD billion) | % of GDP | Amount (USD billion) | % of GDP | Amount (USD billion) | % share | % of GDP | q-o-q | y-o-y |
| **People's Republic of China** | | | | | | | | | |
| Total | 21,252 | 115.0 | 24,000 | 123.1 | 25,002 | 100.0 | 124.5 | 2.2 | 12.6 |
| Treasury and Other Government | 14,440 | 78.1 | 16,604 | 85.2 | 17,290 | 69.2 | 86.1 | 2.2 | 14.6 |
| Central Bank | 2 | 0.01 | 0 | 0.0 | 0 | 0.0 | 0.0 | – | (100.0) |
| Corporate | 6,810 | 36.8 | 7,396 | 37.9 | 7,712 | 30.8 | 38.4 | 2.3 | 8.4 |
| **Hong Kong, China** | | | | | | | | | |
| Total | 402 | 98.0 | 445 | 105.2 | 473 | 100.0 | 110.4 | 6.3 | 17.8 |
| Treasury and Other Government | 39 | 9.5 | 33 | 7.8 | 41 | 8.7 | 9.6 | 24.4 | 5.5 |
| Central Bank | 168 | 41.0 | 171 | 40.5 | 172 | 36.5 | 40.3 | 0.8 | 2.7 |
| Corporate | 195 | 47.5 | 241 | 56.9 | 259 | 54.8 | 60.6 | 7.8 | 33.3 |
| **Indonesia** | | | | | | | | | |
| Total | 477 | 34.7 | 476 | 34.0 | 483 | 100.0 | 33.9 | 1.6 | 4.9 |
| Treasury and Other Government | 387 | 28.1 | 398 | 28.4 | 404 | 83.7 | 28.3 | 1.7 | 8.4 |
| Central Bank | 61 | 4.5 | 47 | 3.3 | 47 | 9.7 | 3.3 | (0.1) | (21.1) |
| Corporate | 29 | 2.1 | 31 | 2.2 | 32 | 6.7 | 2.3 | 3.9 | 13.9 |
| **Republic of Korea** | | | | | | | | | |
| Total | 2,241 | 129.0 | 2,456 | 131.4 | 2,428 | 100.0 | 130.0 | 1.4 | 6.0 |
| Treasury and Other Government | 847 | 48.8 | 972 | 52.0 | 953 | 39.3 | 51.0 | 0.6 | 10.1 |
| Central Bank | 79 | 4.5 | 75 | 4.0 | 75 | 3.1 | 4.0 | 2.5 | (7.2) |
| Corporate | 1,315 | 75.7 | 1,409 | 75.4 | 1,400 | 57.7 | 74.9 | 1.9 | 4.2 |
| **Malaysia** | | | | | | | | | |
| Total | 468 | 126.8 | 530 | 130.7 | 554 | 100.0 | 129.5 | 0.8 | 7.4 |
| Treasury and Other Government | 273 | 73.9 | 307 | 75.7 | 320 | 57.8 | 74.9 | 0.5 | 6.6 |
| Central Bank | 0 | 0.0 | 0 | 0.0 | 0 | 0.0 | 0.0 | – | – |
| Corporate | 195 | 52.9 | 223 | 55.0 | 234 | 42.2 | 54.7 | 1.1 | 8.6 |
| **Philippines** | | | | | | | | | |
| Total | 223 | 48.9 | 237 | 49.8 | 233 | 100.0 | 48.9 | (0.7) | 6.0 |
| Treasury and Other Government | 187 | 40.8 | 203 | 42.7 | 203 | 87.3 | 42.7 | 1.2 | 10.9 |
| Central Bank | 14 | 3.0 | 10 | 2.2 | 6 | 2.5 | 1.2 | (43.6) | (56.4) |
| Corporate | 23 | 5.1 | 23 | 4.9 | 24 | 10.2 | 5.0 | 2.1 | 2.7 |
| **Singapore** | | | | | | | | | |
| Total | 622 | 111.0 | 695 | 114.9 | 698 | 100.0 | 113.6 | 0.03 | 5.6 |
| Treasury and Other Government | 225 | 40.2 | 257 | 42.4 | 257 | 36.9 | 41.9 | (0.1) | 7.6 |
| Central Bank | 249 | 44.5 | 276 | 45.6 | 276 | 39.6 | 45.0 | (0.3) | 4.3 |
| Corporate | 148 | 26.4 | 163 | 26.9 | 164 | 23.5 | 26.7 | 0.7 | 4.6 |
| **Thailand** | | | | | | | | | |
| Total | 501 | 91.4 | 544 | 93.4 | 566 | 100.0 | 94.0 | 1.1 | 4.5 |
| Treasury and Other Government | 297 | 54.1 | 328 | 56.2 | 341 | 60.2 | 56.6 | 1.1 | 6.2 |
| Central Bank | 69 | 12.5 | 79 | 13.6 | 84 | 14.9 | 14.0 | 3.2 | 13.6 |
| Corporate | 136 | 24.7 | 137 | 23.5 | 141 | 24.9 | 23.4 | (0.1) | (4.0) |
| **Viet Nam** | | | | | | | | | |
| Total | 124 | 27.5 | 136 | 28.9 | 151 | 100.0 | 30.9 | 10.5 | 25.6 |
| Treasury and Other Government | 87 | 19.3 | 93 | 19.6 | 97 | 64.3 | 19.9 | 4.5 | 15.1 |
| Central Bank | 5 | 1.2 | 7 | 1.5 | 15 | 9.7 | 3.0 | 107.5 | 178.7 |
| Corporate | 32 | 7.0 | 37 | 7.8 | 39 | 26.0 | 8.0 | 7.0 | 28.6 |
| **Emerging East Asia** | | | | | | | | | |
| Total | 26,311 | 107.9 | 29,520 | 114.7 | 30,588 | 100.0 | 115.8 | 2.1 | 11.6 |
| Treasury and Other Government | 16,781 | 68.8 | 19,195 | 74.6 | 19,908 | 65.1 | 75.4 | 2.0 | 13.8 |
| Central Bank | 646 | 2.7 | 665 | 2.6 | 674 | 2.2 | 2.6 | 1.2 | 1.2 |
| Corporate | 8,883 | 36.4 | 9,660 | 37.5 | 10,006 | 32.7 | 37.9 | 2.3 | 8.1 |
| **Japan** | | | | | | | | | |
| Total | 8,853 | 219.4 | 9,536 | 214.7 | 9,037 | 100.0 | 213.7 | 0.4 | 1.8 |
| Treasury and Other Government | 8,154 | 202.1 | 8,771 | 197.4 | 8,322 | 92.1 | 196.8 | 0.5 | 1.7 |
| Central Bank | 20 | 0.5 | 20 | 0.4 | 7 | 0.1 | 0.2 | (61.2) | (64.3) |
| Corporate | 678 | 16.8 | 745 | 16.8 | 708 | 7.8 | 16.7 | 0.6 | 4.0 |

( ) = negative, – = not applicable, GDP = gross domestic product, Q3 = third quarter, Q4 = fourth quarter, q-o-q = quarter-on-quarter, USD = United States dollar, y-o-y = year-on-year.

Notes:

1. Emerging East Asia is defined to include the member states of ASEAN plus the People's Republic of China; Hong Kong, China; and the Republic of Korea.
2. For Singapore, corporate bonds outstanding are based on *AsianBondsOnline* estimates.
3. Growth rates are calculated from a local currency base and do not include currency effects. For emerging East Asia, growth figures are based on 31 December 2025 currency exchange rates and do not include currency effects.
4. GDP data are from CEIC Data Company. GDP data are as of end-September 2025 for the Republic of Korea.
5. Bloomberg LP end-of-period local currency–USD rates are used.

Sources: People's Republic of China (CEIC Data Company); Hong Kong, China (Hong Kong Monetary Authority); European Union 20 (European Central Bank); Indonesia (Bank Indonesia; Directorate General of Budget Financing and Risk Management, Ministry of Finance; and Indonesia Stock Exchange); Republic of Korea (Bank of Korea and KG Zeroin Corporation); Malaysia (Bank Negara Malaysia); Philippines (Bangko Sentral ng Pilipinas, Bureau of the Treasury and Bloomberg LP); Singapore (Monetary Authority Singapore and Bloomberg LP); Thailand (Bank of Thailand and Thai Bond Market Association); United States (Securities Industry and Financial Markets Association and Bloomberg LP); and Viet Nam (Hanoi Stock Exchange, State Bank of Vietnam, Vietnam Bond Market Association, and Bloomberg LP).

**Table A2: Local-Currency-Denominated Bond Issuance**

| | Q4 2024 | | Q3 2025 | | Q4 2025 | | Growth Rate (%) Q4 2025 | |
|---|---|---|---|---|---|---|---|---|
| | Amount (USD billion) | % share | Amount (USD billion) | % share | Amount (USD billion) | % share | q-o-q | y-o-y |
| **People's Republic of China** | | | | | | | | |
| Total | 1,652 | 100.0 | 2,106 | 100.0 | 1,811 | 100.0 | (15.6) | 5.0 |
| Treasury and Other Government | 953 | 57.7 | 1,253 | 59.5 | 988 | 54.6 | (22.6) | (0.7) |
| Central Bank | 0 | 0.0 | 0 | 0.0 | 0 | 0.0 | – | – |
| Corporate | 699 | 42.3 | 853 | 40.5 | 823 | 45.4 | (5.4) | 12.7 |
| **Hong Kong, China** | | | | | | | | |
| Total | 181 | 100.0 | 203 | 100.0 | 211 | 100.0 | 4.0 | 16.9 |
| Treasury and Other Government | 11 | 5.9 | 0.9 | 0.5 | 8 | 3.9 | 793.1 | (22.2) |
| Central Bank | 134 | 74.3 | 138 | 68.0 | 150 | 71.1 | 8.7 | 11.9 |
| Corporate | 36 | 19.8 | 64 | 32 | 53 | 25.0 | (17.7) | 47.4 |
| **Indonesia** | | | | | | | | |
| Total | 46 | 100.0 | 55 | 100.0 | 55 | 100.0 | (0.1) | 25.3 |
| Treasury and Other Government | 14 | 31.6 | 19 | 34.0 | 14 | 25.8 | (24.3) | 2.5 |
| Central Bank | 28 | 61.5 | 32 | 58.6 | 37 | 67.9 | 15.7 | 38.2 |
| Corporate | 3 | 6.9 | 4 | 7.4 | 4 | 6.3 | (13.9) | 14.8 |
| **Republic of Korea** | | | | | | | | |
| Total | 194 | 100.0 | 207 | 100.0 | 209 | 100.0 | 3.4 | 5.5 |
| Treasury and Other Government | 28 | 14.4 | 62 | 30.1 | 42 | 20.3 | (30.4) | 48.2 |
| Central Bank | 14 | 7.4 | 18 | 8.6 | 17 | 8.0 | (3.5) | 14.6 |
| Corporate | 151 | 78.2 | 127 | 61.3 | 150 | 71.7 | 21.0 | (3.2) |
| **Malaysia** | | | | | | | | |
| Total | 18 | 100.0 | 31 | 100.0 | 27 | 100.0 | (14.5) | 36.7 |
| Treasury and Other Government | 7 | 39.2 | 13 | 43.6 | 8 | 31.4 | (38.4) | 9.5 |
| Central Bank | 0 | 0.0 | 0 | 0.0 | 0 | 0.0 | – | – |
| Corporate | 11 | 60.8 | 17 | 56.4 | 19 | 68.6 | 4.0 | 54.2 |
| **Philippines** | | | | | | | | |
| Total | 41 | 100.0 | 50 | 100.0 | 30 | 100.0 | (39.8) | (26.2) |
| Treasury and Other Government | 7 | 17.7 | 22 | 43.6 | 9 | 31.6 | (56.4) | 31.9 |
| Central Bank | 33 | 79.7 | 24 | 49.0 | 19 | 62.4 | (23.3) | (42.2) |
| Corporate | 1 | 2.6 | 4 | 7.4 | 2 | 5.9 | (51.5) | 70.4 |
| **Singapore** | | | | | | | | |
| Total | 411 | 100.0 | 443 | 100.0 | 433 | 100.0 | (2.6) | (0.8) |
| Treasury and Other Government | 40 | 9.8 | 51 | 11.5 | 50 | 11.4 | (3.3) | 16.2 |
| Central Bank | 367 | 89.4 | 385 | 86.8 | 380 | 87.7 | (1.6) | (2.7) |
| Corporate | 3 | 0.8 | 8 | 1.7 | 4 | 0.9 | (50.5) | 3.1 |
| **Thailand** | | | | | | | | |
| Total | 61 | 100.0 | 69 | 100.0 | 70 | 100.0 | (0.9) | 6.3 |
| Treasury and Other Government | 18 | 29.0 | 16 | 23.0 | 15 | 22.0 | (5.3) | (19.2) |
| Central Bank | 33 | 54.4 | 42 | 60.4 | 43 | 61.2 | 0.4 | 19.7 |
| Corporate | 10 | 16.6 | 11 | 16.6 | 12 | 16.8 | 0.2 | 7.2 |
| **Viet Nam** | | | | | | | | |
| Total | 37 | 100.0 | 48 | 100.0 | 44 | 100.0 | (7.6) | 25.2 |
| Treasury and Other Government | 2 | 6.3 | 2 | 4.3 | 5 | 10.4 | 124.4 | 107.6 |
| Central Bank | 30 | 82.7 | 42 | 87.8 | 35 | 78.8 | (17.1) | 19.3 |
| Corporate | 4 | 11.0 | 4 | 7.9 | 5 | 10.8 | 26.5 | 22.5 |
| **Emerging East Asia** | | | | | | | | |
| Total | 2,639 | 100.0 | 3,212 | 100.0 | 2,891 | 100.0 | (11.1) | 5.3 |
| Treasury and Other Government | 1,080 | 40.9 | 1,439 | 44.8 | 1,141 | 39.5 | (22.0) | 1.2 |
| Central Bank | 640 | 24.3 | 681 | 21.2 | 681 | 23.5 | (0.3) | 2.6 |
| Corporate | 919 | 34.8 | 1,092 | 34.0 | 1,070 | 37.0 | (3.3) | 12.0 |
| **Japan** | | | | | | | | |
| Total | 340 | 100.0 | 349 | 100.0 | 339 | 100.0 | 3.2 | (0.5) |
| Treasury and Other Government | 301 | 88.6 | 315 | 90.3 | 310 | 91.4 | 4.4 | 2.7 |
| Central Bank | 11 | 3.2 | 0 | 0.0 | 0 | 0.0 | – | (100.0) |
| Corporate | 28 | 8.2 | 34 | 9.7 | 29 | 8.6 | (8.0) | 4.0 |

( ) = negative, – = not applicable, Q3 = third quarter, Q4 = fourth quarter, q-o-q = quarter-on-quarter, USD = United States dollar, y-o-y = year-on-year.

Notes:
1. Data reflect gross bond issuance.
2. Bloomberg LP end-of-period local currency–USD rates are used.
3. Growth rates are calculated from a local currency base and do not include currency effects. For emerging East Asia, growth figures are based on 31 December 2025 currency exchange rates and do not include currency effects.

Sources: People's Republic of China (CEIC Data Company); Hong Kong, China (Hong Kong Monetary Authority); Indonesia (Bank Indonesia, Directorate General of Budget Financing and Risk Management, Ministry of Finance; and Indonesia Stock Exchange); Japan (Japan Securities Dealers Association); Republic of Korea (Bank of Korea and KG Zeroin Corporation); Malaysia (Bank Negara Malaysia); Philippines (Bangko Sentral ng Pilipinas, Bureau of the Treasury and Bloomberg LP); Singapore (Monetary Authority of Singapore and Bloomberg LP); Thailand (Bank of Thailand and Thai Bond Market Association); and Viet Nam (Hanoi Stock Exchange, State Bank of Vietnam, Vietnam Bond Market Association, and Bloomberg LP).

# Recent Developments in the ASEAN+3 Sustainable Bond Market

**The ASEAN+3 sustainable bond market posted a robust expansion in 2025, driven by increased issuance amid generally accommodative monetary stances.**[13] At the end of December, ASEAN+3's sustainable bonds outstanding recorded USD1.0 trillion, expanding 10.4% year-on-year (y-o-y) from USD0.9 billion in 2024 (**Figure 11A**). This gain was supported by record issuance of USD275.9 billion amid an accommodative monetary stance in most regional economies, although the pace of expansion moderated from 12.5% y-o-y in 2024 due to a larger volume of bond maturities in 2025 (USD179.6 billion) than in the previous year (USD137.9 billion). ASEAN+3 accounted for 18.5% of global sustainable bonds outstanding (USD5.5 trillion) at the end of 2025, making it the world's second-largest regional sustainable bond market after the European Union 20 (EU-20).[14] Issuance in the ASEAN+3 sustainable bond market (USD275.9 billion) led all regions in 2025, raising its share of global sustainable bond issuance to 29.8% from 24.0% in 2024 and exceeding the EU-20's 2025 issuance share of 29.3% (**Figure 11B**).

## Market Profile

**ASEAN economies and the Republic of Korea have higher shares of bonds outstanding in the ASEAN+3 sustainable bond market than in the ASEAN+3 general bond market.** Supported by easing monetary stances, ASEAN sustainable bonds outstanding expanded at the fastest rate (29.5% y-o-y) across ASEAN+3 to reach

**Figure 11: Global Sustainable Bonds Outstanding and Issuances in 2025**

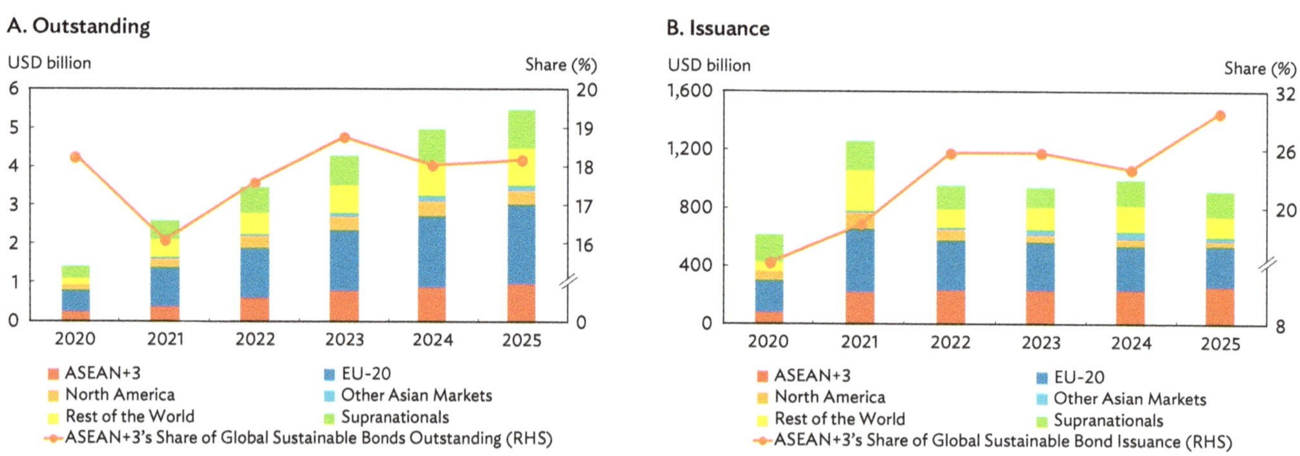


ASEAN = Association of Southeast Asian Nations, EU-20 = European Union 20; RHS = right-hand side, USD = United States dollar.

Notes:

1. ASEAN+3 comprises the member states of the Association of Southeast Asian Nations (ASEAN) plus the People's Republic of China; Hong Kong, China; Japan; and the Republic of Korea.
2. The EU-20 includes European Union member markets Austria, Belgium, Croatia, Cyprus, Estonia, Finland, France, Germany, Greece, Ireland, Italy, Latvia, Lithuania, Luxembourg, Malta, the Netherlands, Portugal, Slovakia, Slovenia, and Spain.
3. Data include both local currency and foreign currency sustainable bonds.

Source: *AsianBondsOnline* calculations based on Bloomberg LP data.

[13] ASEAN+3 comprises the member states of the Association of Southeast Asian Nations (ASEAN) plus the People's Republic of China; Hong Kong, China; Japan; and the Republic of Korea.

[14] The EU-20 includes European Union member markets Austria, Belgium, Croatia, Cyprus, Estonia, Finland, France, Germany, Greece, Ireland, Italy, Latvia, Lithuania, Luxembourg, Malta, the Netherlands, Portugal, Slovakia, Slovenia, and Spain.

USD121.4 billion at the end of 2025. This lifted ASEAN's share of ASEAN+3 sustainable bonds outstanding to 11.9%, more than double its share of 5.9% in the ASEAN+3 general bond market, from 10.2% in 2024. The People's Republic of China (PRC) continued to lead ASEAN+3's sustainable bond market, accounting for 40.2% of sustainable bonds outstanding at the end of 2025. However, this was less than its corresponding share in the ASEAN+3 general bond market (58.3%). Japan's sustainable bonds outstanding comprised 24.8% of the regional total at the end of 2025, which was broadly similar with its share in the ASEAN+3 general bond market (29.6%). Bonds from the Republic of Korea had a more significant presence in the ASEAN+3 sustainable bond market (18.5%) than in the region's general bond market (5.5%). By market, the PRC accounted for 60.5% of the regional green bond total while Japan comprised 89.7% of the transition bond total (**Figure 12A**).

**ASEAN+3 sustainable bond issuance in 2025 was buoyed by increased issuance from the PRC and ASEAN economies.** Sustainable bond issuance in the PRC rose 54.8% y-o-y in 2025 following a contraction of 3.7% y-o-y in 2024, spurred by financial sector issuances amid the PRC's push for sustainable development under its 14th 5-Year Plan for a Modern Energy System, 2021–2025.[15] The PRC remained the largest issuer of sustainable bonds in ASEAN+3 in 2025 with aggregate issuance of USD147.8 billion, comprising 53.6% of the regional total. ASEAN markets contributed 11.9% of ASEAN+3's total issuance and accounted for most of the region's issuance of sustainability-linked bonds (57.9%). In ASEAN, a sizable share of issuance came from the public sector, partly driven by regular issuances through Treasury auction plans in some markets. Among ASEAN economies, the share of public sector issuances in 2025 was the highest for Thailand (79.5%), Indonesia (67.1%), and Singapore (56.7%). Meanwhile, Japan and the Republic of Korea, which accounted for 16.2% and 16.0% of regional sustainable bond issuance, respectively, were the most active issuers of transition bonds (Japan, 90.2%) and social bonds (Republic of Korea, 61.6%) (**Figure 12B**).

## Instrument Profile

**ASEAN+3's sustainable bond market has a more diverse instrument profile than the EU-20's market.** Green bonds accounted for 57.1% of ASEAN+3's sustainable bonds outstanding at the end of 2025, down from 59.0% a year earlier (**Figure 13A**). Social bonds' share decreased to 18.8% from 19.2% during the same period. The collective share of sustainability, sustainability-linked, and transition bonds rose to 24.1%

**Figure 12: Market Profile of ASEAN+3 Sustainable Bonds Outstanding and Issuance Across Different Bond Types in 2025**

**A. Outstanding** **B. Issuance**

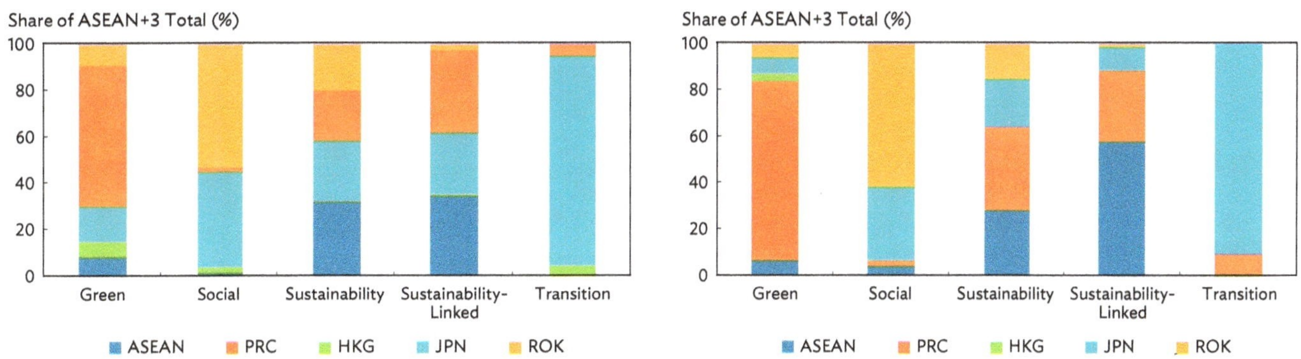


ASEAN = Association of Southeast Asian Nations; PRC = People's Republic of China; HKG = Hong Kong, China; JPN = Japan; ROK = Republic of Korea.

Notes:

1. ASEAN+3 comprises the member states of the Association of Southeast Asian Nations (ASEAN) plus the People's Republic of China; Hong Kong, China; Japan; and the Republic of Korea.
2. ASEAN comprises the markets of Cambodia, Indonesia, the Lao People's Democratic Republic, Malaysia, the Philippines, Singapore, Thailand, and Viet Nam.
3. Sustainability-linked bonds include transition-linked bonds.
4. Data include both local currency and foreign currency sustainable bonds.

Source: *AsianBondsOnline* computations based on Bloomberg LP data.

[15] Released in 2022, the plan included targets such as reducing greenhouse gases by 18% and raising the proportion of non-fossil fuels to 20% of energy consumption by the end of 2025.

**Figure 13: Instrument Profile of ASEAN+3's Sustainable Bonds Outstanding and Issuance**

**A. ASEAN+3 Sustainable Bonds Outstanding, 2020–2025** **B. Instrument Profile of Sustainable Bond Issuance in 2025**

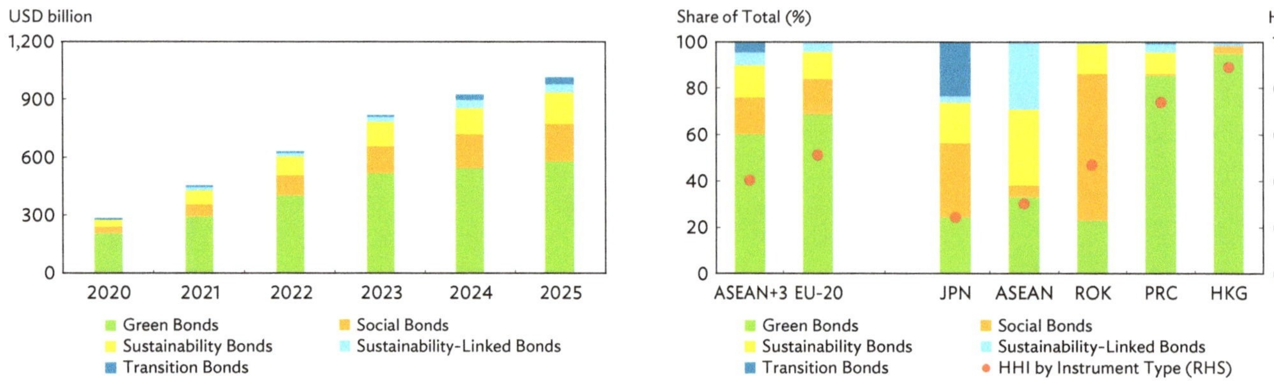


ASEAN+3 = Association of Southeast Asian Nations plus the People's Republic of China; Hong Kong, China; Japan; and the Republic of Korea; EU-20 = European Union 20; HHI = Herfindahl–Hirschman Index, RHS = right-hand side; USD = United States dollar.

Notes:

1. Figures are based on the outstanding amount for each instrument type relative to the regional total of sustainable bonds outstanding.
2. The EU-20 includes European Union member markets Austria, Belgium, Croatia, Cyprus, Estonia, Finland, France, Germany, Greece, Ireland, Italy, Latvia, Lithuania, Luxembourg, Malta, the Netherlands, Portugal, Slovakia, Slovenia, and Spain.
3. The Herfindahl–Hirschman Index is a commonly accepted measure of market concentration. The index is used to measure the instrument profile diversification of bond markets and is calculated by summing the squared share of each instrument type in the market. A lower HHI indicates greater diversification across different instrument types, while a higher HHI suggests a more concentrated market structure dominated by fewer instruments.
4. Data include both local currency and foreign currency sustainable bonds.

Source: *AsianBondsOnline* calculations based on Bloomberg LP data.

in 2025 from 21.7% in 2024, as growth in sustainability-linked bond issuance accelerated to 50.5% y-o-y in 2025 from 14.1% y-o-y in 2024, led mainly by ASEAN members, particularly Thailand as part of its commitment to climate change mitigation following the release of a Sustainability-Linked Financing Framework in October 2024. Green bonds comprised 59.6% of ASEAN+3 sustainable bond issuance in 2025. This was less than the corresponding share of 69.1% in the EU-20, leading to a more diversified instrument profile in ASEAN+3 as captured by the Herfindahl–Hirschman Index (**Figure 13B**).[16]

## Sector Profile

**The ASEAN+3 sustainable bond market was buttressed in 2025 by strong private capital mobilization.** Private sector bonds continued to dominate ASEAN+3's sustainable bond market in 2025, accounting for 68.7% of total sustainable bonds outstanding at the end of December, compared with 51.4% in the EU-20 (**Figure 14**). The private sector's share in ASEAN+3 sustainable bond issuance in 2025 was 70.2%, which was also higher than in the EU-20 (63.9%). Over 90%

**Figure 14: Public and Private Sector Shares of ASEAN+3 Sustainable Bonds Outstanding by Market and Instrument Type in 2025**

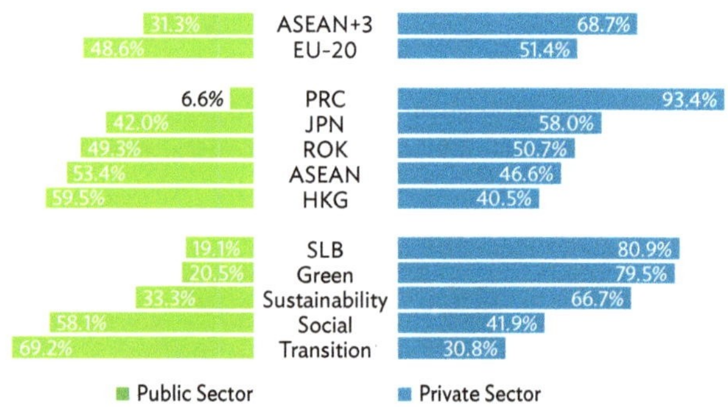


ASEAN = Association of Southeast Asian Nations; PRC = People's Republic of China; EU-20 = European Union 20; HKG = Hong Kong, China; JPN = Japan; ROK = Republic of Korea; SLB = sustainability-linked bond.

Notes:

1. ASEAN+3 is defined to include member states of the Association of Southeast Asian Nations (ASEAN) plus the People's Republic of China; Hong Kong, China; Japan; and the Republic of Korea.
2. The EU-20 includes European Union member markets Austria, Belgium, Croatia, Cyprus, Estonia, Finland, France, Germany, Greece, Ireland, Italy, Latvia, Lithuania, Luxembourg, Malta, the Netherlands, Portugal, Slovakia, Slovenia, and Spain.
3. Data include both local currency and foreign currency sustainable bonds.
4. The private sector includes financial institutions and private institutions, while excluding government-owned enterprises.
5. SLBs include transition-linked bonds.

Source: *AsianBondsOnline* computations based on Bloomberg LP data.

[15] The Herfindahl–Hirschman Index is a commonly accepted measure of market concentration. The index is used to measure the instrument profile diversification of a bond market and is calculated by summing the squared share of each instrument type in the market. A lower HHI indicates greater diversification across different instrument types, while a higher HHI suggests a more concentrated market structure dominated by fewer instruments.

of sustainable bond issuance in the PRC came from the private sector in 2025, while the share of public sector issuance was highest in the region in Hong Kong, China (64.5%) and the Republic of Korea (62.5%). Financial institutions were the major financers in ASEAN+3's private sustainable bond markets in 2025, accounting for 53.9% of ASEAN+3 private sector sustainable bond issuance in 2025, leading the issuance of green (61.7%), social (49.4%), and sustainability (35.6%) bonds. Utilities were the most active issuers of transition bonds (44.7%) in ASEAN+3 (**Figure 15**). In the EU-20, about half of its private sector issuance in 2025 came from financial institutions (51.5%), followed by utilities (27.4%).

**Figure 15: ASEAN+3 Sustainable Bond Issuance by Sector and Type of Bond in 2025**

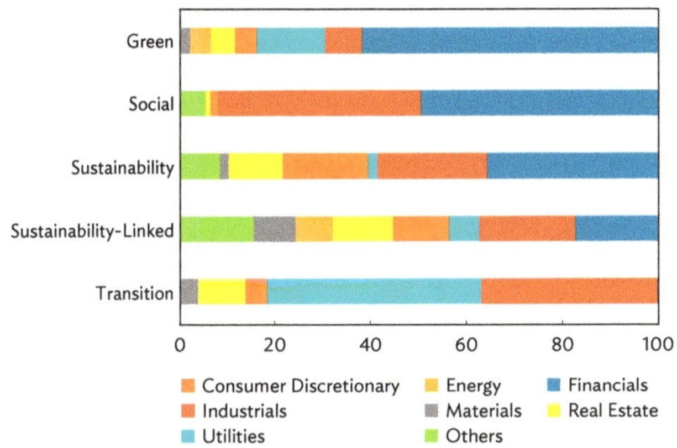


Notes:
1. ASEAN+3 is defined to include member states of the Association of Southeast Asian Nations (ASEAN) plus the People's Republic of China; Hong Kong, China; Japan; and the Republic of Korea.
2. Data include both local currency and foreign currency sustainable bonds.

Source: *AsianBondsOnline* computations based on Bloomberg LP data.

## Currency Profile

**While local currency (LCY) financing was prevalent in ASEAN+3's sustainable bond market in 2025, it still had a relatively smaller presence than LCY financing in the region's general bond market.** LCY financing comprised 73.4% of total sustainable bonds outstanding and 78.4% of sustainable bond issuance in ASEAN+3 in 2025, compared with LCY financing shares of 95.4% and 94.2% for ASEAN+3 general bonds outstanding and issuance, respectively (**Figure 16A**). This contrasts with the EU-20 bond market, where LCY financing shares are similar in both the sustainable and general bond markets. In the EU-20, LCY financing accounted for 90.9% of sustainable bonds outstanding at the end of 2025, very similar to the LCY financing share of 91.0% in its general bond market. In terms of issuance, LCY issuance shares were relatively similar for the sustainable bond (87.7%)

**Figure 16: Local Currency Share in ASEAN+3 Sustainable Bonds Outstanding and Issuance by Market and Instrument Type in 2025**

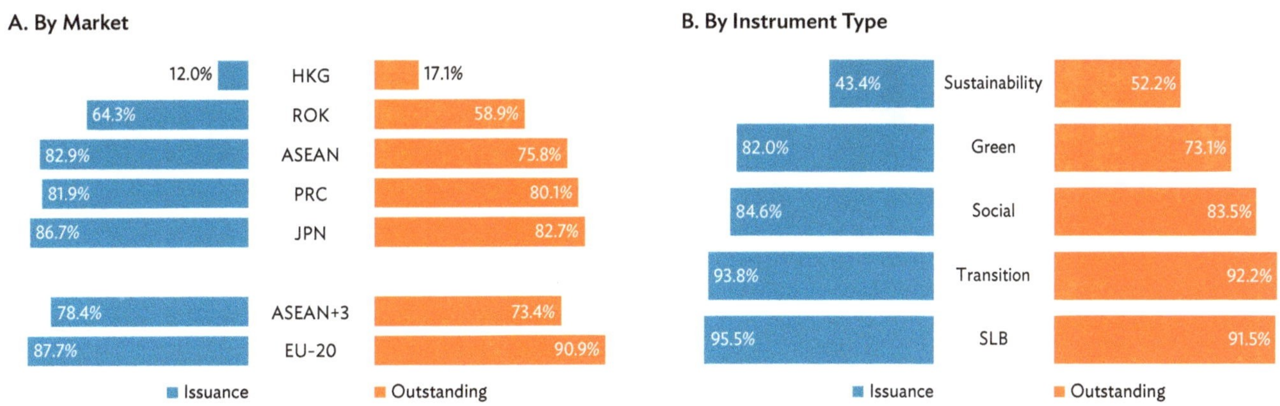


ASEAN = Association of Southeast Asian Nations; PRC = People's Republic of China; EU-20 = European Union 20; HKG = Hong Kong, China; JPN = Japan; ROK = Republic of Korea; SLB = sustainability-linked bond.

Notes:
1. ASEAN+3 is defined to include member states of the Association of Southeast Asian Nations (ASEAN) plus the People's Republic of China; Hong Kong, China; Japan; and the Republic of Korea.
2. ASEAN comprises the markets of Cambodia, Indonesia, the Lao People's Democratic Republic, Malaysia, the Philippines, Singapore, Thailand, and Viet Nam.
3. The EU-20 includes European Union member markets Austria, Belgium, Croatia, Cyprus, Estonia, Finland, France, Germany, Greece, Ireland, Italy, Latvia, Lithuania, Luxembourg, Malta, the Netherlands, Portugal, Slovakia, Slovenia, and Spain.
4. Data include both local currency and foreign currency sustainable bonds.

Source: *AsianBondsOnline* computations based on Bloomberg LP data.

and general bond (87.6%) markets in the EU-20. Within ASEAN+3, ASEAN members had a slightly higher average LCY financing share in 2025 for sustainable bond market issuance (82.9%) than for general bond market issuance (77.9%) due to significant private sector issuance of LCY-denominated sustainable bonds. Among different types of bond instruments, the LCY financing share was highest in ASEAN+3 for sustainability-linked bonds (95.5%), driven by ASEAN markets. The next highest LCY financing share was for transition bonds (93.8%), led by Japan (**Figure 16B**).

## Maturity Profile

**Sustainable bonds in ASEAN+3 carried shorter maturities, on average, than those in the EU-20.** At the end of 2025, 73.2% of sustainable bonds outstanding and 80.2% of annual sustainable bond issuance in ASEAN+3 carried tenors of 5 years or less, much higher than the EU-20's corresponding shares of 45.1% and 31.4% (**Figure 17**). Thus, the size-weighted average maturity of sustainable bond issuance in ASEAN+3 in 2025 was 5.1 years, notably shorter than the corresponding averages for the EU-20 (8.4 years) and ASEAN (9.8 years). This was mostly due to a higher share of private sector financing in the ASEAN+3 sustainable bond market, which generally issues short-term bonds as investors avoid the risks involved in buying long-term corporate bonds. On the other hand, the public sector tends to issue more long-term sustainable bonds. ASEAN+3's public sector sustainable bonds outstanding at the end of 2025 had a size-weighted average tenor of 7.0 years, compared to 3.4 years in the private sector (**Figure 18**). ASEAN markets had a relatively high share of sustainable bonds outstanding with tenors of 10 years or above (34.0%), driven by the share of public sector sustainable bonds outstanding with these long-term tenors (55.0%). Thus, sustainable bonds outstanding in ASEAN markets had a size-weighted average tenor of 10.4 years, longer than the corresponding averages for both ASEAN+3 (4.5 years) and the EU-20 (8.0 years).

**Figure 17: Tenor Profiles of ASEAN+3 and EU-20 Sustainable Bonds Outstanding by Type of Bond at the End of 2025**

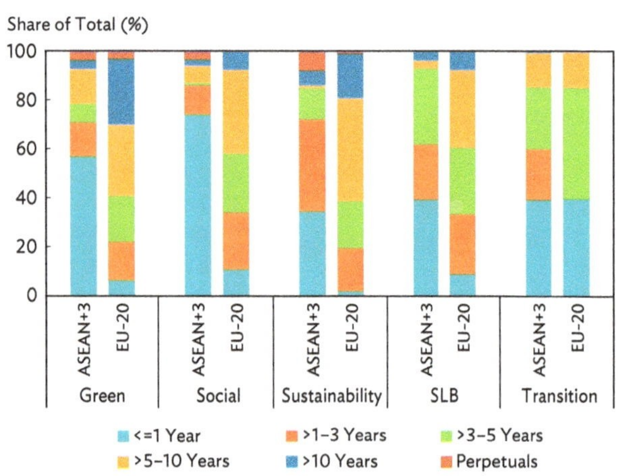


ASEAN+3 = Association of Southeast Asian Nations plus the People's Republic of China; Hong Kong, China; Japan; and the Republic of Korea; EU-20 = European Union 20; SLB = sustainability-linked bond.

Notes:

1. The EU-20 includes EU member markets Austria, Belgium, Croatia, Cyprus, Estonia, Finland, France, Germany, Greece, Ireland, Italy, Latvia, Lithuania, Luxembourg, Malta, the Netherlands, Portugal, Slovakia, Slovenia, and Spain.
2. Data include both local currency and foreign currency sustainable bonds.
3. SLBs include transition-linked bonds.

Source: *AsianBondsOnline* computations based on Bloomberg LP data.

**Figure 18: Tenor Profiles of ASEAN+3 and EU-20 Sustainable Bonds Outstanding by Sector at the End of 2025**

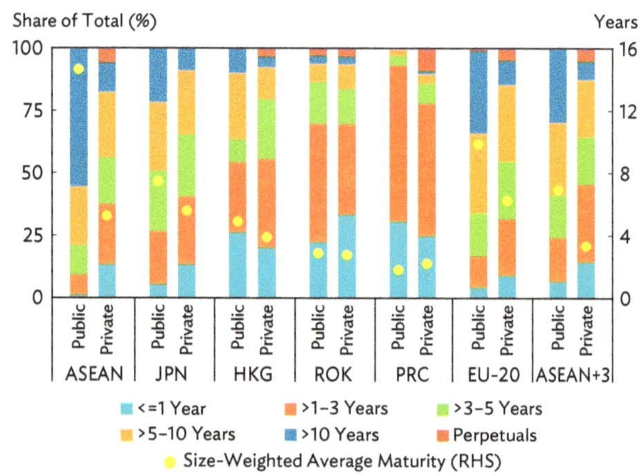


ASEAN = Association of Southeast Asian Nations; PRC = People's Republic of China; HKG = Hong Kong, China; JPN = Japan; RHS = right-hand side; ROK = Republic of Korea; EU-20 = European Union 20.

Notes:

1. ASEAN+3 is defined to include member states of ASEAN plus the People's Republic of China; Hong Kong, China; Japan; and the Republic of Korea.
2. ASEAN comprises the markets of Cambodia, Indonesia, the Lao People's Democratic Republic, Malaysia, the Philippines, Singapore, Thailand, and Viet Nam.
3. The EU-20 includes EU member markets Austria, Belgium, Croatia, Cyprus, Estonia, Finland, France, Germany, Greece, Ireland, Italy, Latvia, Lithuania, Luxembourg, Malta, the Netherlands, Portugal, Slovakia, Slovenia, and Spain.
4. Data include both local currency and foreign currency sustainable bonds.

Source: *AsianBondsOnline* computations based on Bloomberg LP data.

# Policy and Regulatory Developments

## People's Republic of China

### People's Bank of China Conducts Targeted Central Bank Lending and Discount Rate Cuts

On 15 January, the People's Bank of China reduced by 25 basis points the central bank lending and discount rates, effective 19 January. The rate reduction is only applicable to bank lending for rural development and to micro and small businesses. The effective lending rate will be 0.95%, 1.15%, and 1.25% for the 3-month, 5-month, and 1-year maturities, respectively.

### Ministry of Finance and State Taxation Administration Extend Tax Exemption for Overseas Institutions

On 15 January, the Ministry of Finance and the State Taxation Administration announced they would extend the tax exemption of overseas institutions on the payment of corporate income tax and value-added tax for interest income from bond investments in the People's Republic of China. This exemption will be extended until 31 December 2027.

## Hong Kong, China

### Hong Kong Monetary Authority Launches Phase 2A of Hong Kong Taxonomy for Sustainable Finance, Expanding Coverage to Transition and Climate Adaptation

On 22 January, the Hong Kong Monetary Authority published the Hong Kong Taxonomy for Sustainable Finance Phase 2A, following public consultations in September–October 2025. Phase 2A enhances the original framework, released in May 2024, to (i) cover more economic activities; (ii) add manufacturing and information and communication technology as new sectors; (iii) include transition elements; and (iv) introduce climate change adaptation as a new environmental objective. According to the Hong Kong Monetary Authority, the enhancements to the framework received support from a wide variety of stakeholders.

## Indonesia

### Ministry of Finance to Issue Varying Tenors of Short-Term Securities

In December, the Ministry of Finance of Indonesia announced its plan to increase issuance of short-term securities, particularly for both conventional and Islamic Treasury bills. The issuance will include 1-month, 3-month, 6-month, 9-month, and 12-month Treasury bills. The move was undertaken to further develop and deepen Indonesia's financial markets, as well as to improve the efficiency of cash management.

## Republic of Korea

### The Republic of Korea Announces Tax Reforms to Support Domestic Investment and Foreign Exchange Stability

On 24 December 2025, the Government of the Republic of Korea introduced tax measures to promote domestic investment and support foreign exchange stability. These include the 1-year temporary capital tax gains exemption for investors who sell offshore stock investments and convert the proceeds to Korean won in order to make long-term investments in the domestic equity market. The government will also introduce foreign exchange forward contracts for individual investors and provide capital gains tax exemption for those that avail of these hedging instruments. To address the double taxation on dividend income that domestic parent companies receive from their overseas subsidiaries, the government will raise the income exclusion ratio to 100% from 95%. These tax measures were implemented on 1 January 2026.

### The Republic of Korea Announces Road Map for Inclusion in the MSCI Developed Markets Index

On 9 January, the Government of the Republic of Korea announced the road map for its inclusion in the MSCI Developed Markets Index. It aims to be included in the watch list in the annual market classification review to be conducted in June 2026, with possible inclusion in the developed market index in June 2027. The road map includes, among others, the extension of foreign exchange market operations to 24 hours starting in July from the current hours of 9 a.m. to 2 a.m. the next day. The government will also ease regulations to allow offshore trading of the Korean won and create a settlement system to facilitate this. Other improvements include simplifying registration and account opening requirements for investors and rationalizing short-selling regulations.

## Malaysia

### Malaysia Revises Capital Market Fees Framework

On 1 January, the Securities Commission Malaysia implemented a new payment scheme under the Capital Markets and Services (Fees) Regulations 2025. The reform recalibrates regulatory charges across issuance and licensing activities, with a 3-year transition period (2026–2028) to ensure orderly market adjustment. Among others, the revised payment structure provides a 50% reduction to variable annual fees and a 20% reduction to product and fund-raising activity fees. The measure aims to support the sustainability and integrity of Malaysia's capital market and may affect issuance cost dynamics for bond and *sukuk* (Islamic bond) offerings.

## Philippines

### Bangko Sentral ng Pilipinas Cuts Reserve Requirements for Trust Accounts

On 11 February, the Bangko Sentral ng Pilipinas issued Circular No. 1229, reducing the reserve requirement for trust and other fiduciary accounts to 0% from 17%. The circular also lowered reserve requirements on several other instruments, including (i) bonds issued by universal, commercial, and digital banks (from 3% to 2%); (ii) mortgages or chattel mortgage certificates issued by thrift banks (from 6% to 0%); and (iii) long-term negotiable certificates of time deposits (from 4% to 0%). This reform aims to boost liquidity and reduce intermediation costs for lenders, strengthening the Bangko Sentral ng Pillpinas' efforts to simplify reserve rules and support capital market development. The new regulation will take effect on 27 February.

## Singapore

### Singapore Announces Capital Market Initiatives to Strengthen Financial Ties with the People's Republic of China

On 15 December, Singapore expanded cross-border capital market connectivity through new financial cooperation initiatives with the PRC. This arrangement allows designated banks in Singapore to provide institutional investors access to fixed-income products in the China Interbank Bond Market, strengthening Singapore's role as a regional investment gateway. Furthermore, the appointment of DBS bank as a Chinese yuan (CNY) clearing bank enhances offshore CNY settlement capacity and supports CNY-denominated financing activity. These measures aim to support cross-border bond flows and trading activity while aiding the development of Singapore as a regional fixed-income hub.

## Thailand

### Public Debt Management Office Conducts THB17.3 Billion Electronic Bond Switch

On 21 November, Thailand's Public Debt Management Office completed bond switch transactions amounting to THB17.3 billion. These transactions allowed investors to exchange their holdings of the designated source bond, which will mature in June 2026, to six destination bonds with remaining tenors ranging from 4.3 years to 51.6 years. Bond switch operations support the government's debt management by lengthening the maturity profile of outstanding bonds and increasing the liquidity of longer-term benchmark bonds. The bond swap helps investors manage their portfolios by extending the maturity profile of their holdings and reducing the risk of reinvesting at lower interest rates. Transaction costs are also lower as bond swaps are conducted electronically.

## Viet Nam

### Government Tightens Sanction on Private Placement Violations

On 25 November, the Government of Viet Nam issued Decree No. 306, imposing tougher penalties on violations related to private placements of shares and corporate bonds. The new decree broadens the scope of sanctionable offenses covering the areas of (i) disclosure and documentation requirements, (ii) strict adherence to registration and issuance timelines, (iii) misuse of proceeds, and (iv) stricter rules for investor eligibility and service providers' conduct. Fines range from VND50 million to VND1.5 billion, with the highest penalties applied to violations involving falsified documents and forgery. This policy aims to tighten oversight, enhance market transparency, and strengthen investor protection in the capital market. The new decree took effect on 9 January 2026.

## Government Plans to Borrow VND969.8 Trillion in 2026

In February, the Government of Viet Nam announced its approved borrowing plan of VND969.8 trillion in 2026, about 19% higher than the VND815.2 trillion borrowing plan in 2025. Public debt is forecast to reach 36%–37% of the economy's gross domestic product at the end of 2026, while government and foreign debt is expected at 34%–35% and 32%–33% of gross domestic product, respectively. All ratios remain well below the National Assembly's ceilings of 60% for public debt and 50% each for government and foreign debt. To meet its financing needs, the government will utilize resources such as government bonds, official development assistance, and concessional foreign loans. Viet Nam plans to issue government bonds worth VND500 trillion in 2026.

# Summary of "The Role of Artificial Intelligence in Finance: A Selective Review and Implications for Asia's Financial Stability"

Artificial intelligence (AI) is fundamentally altering the landscape of global finance. By seamlessly integrating predictive analytics with sophisticated automation, it has unlocked new frontiers in data-driven decision-making that were once considered futuristic. "The Role of Artificial Intelligence in Finance: A Selective Review and Implications for Asia's Financial Stability" and its accompanying Appendix present a systematic, data-driven exploration of 249 peer-reviewed studies published between 1990 and 2025. This synthesis examines how AI has revolutionized asset pricing and portfolio management, financial markets and institutions, and corporate finance and governance—culminating in an assessment of its implications for financial stability in Asia. The literature review's dual focus—on empirical applications and systemic consequences—provides both breadth and depth, offering a panoramic view of AI's current and future role in finance.

## Research Scope and Methodology

We employ a quantitative bibliometric and qualitative literature review approach. Using the *Academic Journal Guide* of the United Kingdom's Association of Business Schools, we selected top-tier journals to ensure academic rigor.[16] Search terms were derived from 28 AI-related keywords (e.g., machine learning, neural networks, generative AI, natural language processing [NLP], and explainable AI) and 48 finance-related terms (e.g., asset pricing, corporate governance, systemic risk, credit scoring, and volatility forecasting).

From 94 sources, we identified 249 key publications spanning 1990–2025. **Table 1** summarizes these descriptive statistics, revealing both the maturity and dynamism of AI-finance scholarship. **Figure 19** reveals an exponential increase in publications about AI and finance after 2015, coinciding with the rise of deep learning, NLP, and large language models. This bibliometric surge reflects finance's rapid digital transformation and researchers' growing reliance on AI to decode nonlinear, high-dimensional market relationships.

**Figure 20** portrays AI as a core "intelligence infrastructure" linking three major financial domains: (i) asset pricing and portfolio management, (ii) financial markets and institutions, and (iii) corporate finance and governance—all of which ultimately impact financial stability.

**Table 1: Descriptive Statistics**

| Description | Results |
|---|---|
| **Panel A: Main Data Information** | |
| Timespan | 1990–2025 |
| Sources (journals, books) | 94 |
| Number of Documents | 249 |
| Annual Growth Rate (%) | 10.40 |
| Average Age of Documents | 6.21 |
| Average Number of Citations per Document | 55.46 |
| Number of References | 15,072 |
| **Panel B: Document Contents** | |
| Number of Authors' Keywords | 794 |
| **Panel C: Authors** | |
| Number of Authors | 683 |
| Number of Authors of Single-Authored Docs | 25 |
| Number of Co-Authors per Document | 2.87 |

Source: Authors' compilation.

This special section was written by Yang Zhang (associate professor of Business Economics) at the Faculty of Business Administration, University of Macau; Ziang Qiu (PhD student) at the University of Macau; Donghyun Park (director of Macroeconomics and Monetary Policy Management) at the South East Asian Central Banks Research and Training Centre; and Shu Tian (principal economist) at the Macroeconomics Research Division, Economic Research and Development Impact Department of the Asian Development Bank.

[16] The *Academic Journal Guide* (AJG) aims to assist in navigating the research landscape by providing well-supported, evidence-based information and data. It offers comprehensive details on a variety of journals across disciplines that are significant to business and management studies. The AJG's ratings derive from peer reviews, editorial assessments, and expert judgments, using statistical citation data for guidance. It then evaluates these metrics alongside insights from consultations conducted by the AJG's Scientific Committee, which engages with expert peers and scholarly associations to determine the relative prestige of journals within each field.

**Figure 19: Number of Papers per Journal by Year of Publication**

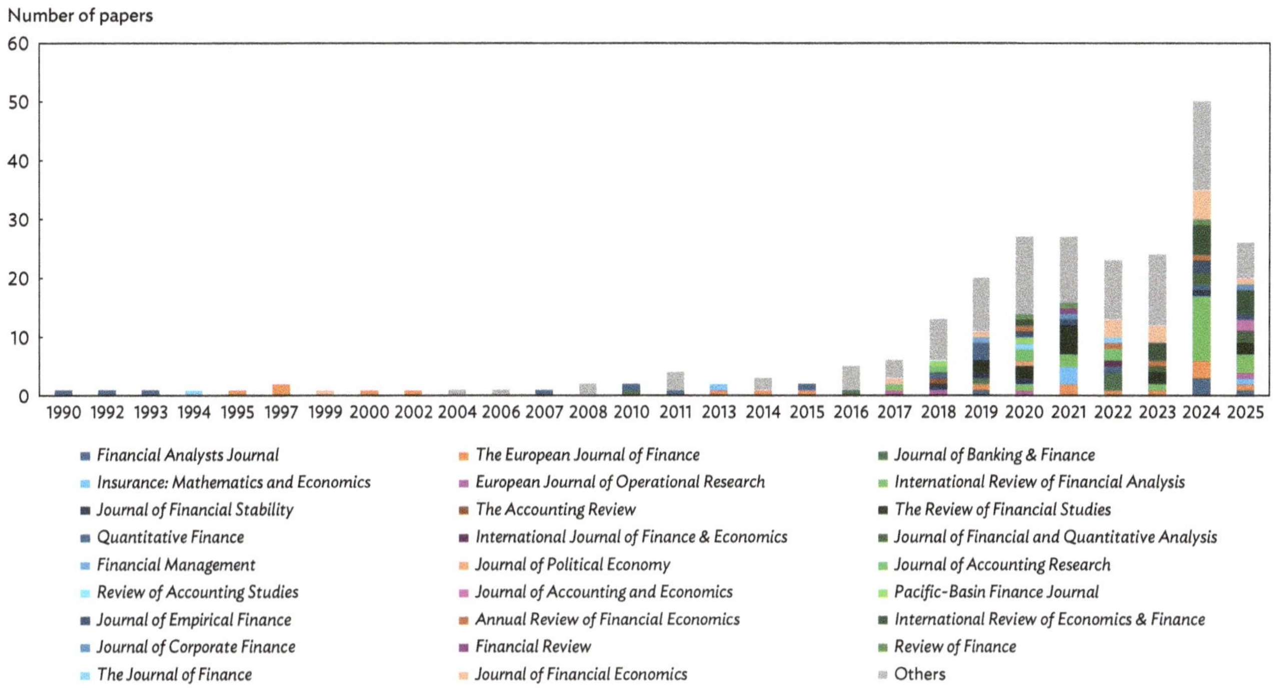


Source: Authors' compilation.

**Figure 20: Conceptual Map of Artificial Intelligence's Roles in Finance**

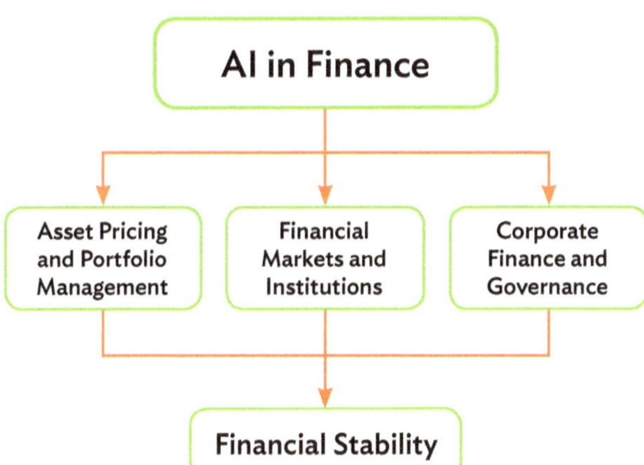


AI = artificial intelligence.
Source: Authors' illustration.

## Artificial Intelligence in Asset Pricing and Portfolio Management

Traditional financial models, such as the capital asset pricing model and Fama–French factors, have long been constrained by linearity assumptions and limited data dimensions. Machine learning has revolutionized this paradigm. Studies like Gu, Kelly, and Xiu (2020) and Freyberger, Neuhierl, and Weber (2020) show that machine learning algorithms capture complex nonlinear relationships between firm characteristics, macroeconomic indicators, and historical returns, while consistently outperforming linear benchmarks.

Neural networks, random forests, and gradient boosting models identify hidden factors and predict equity returns with unprecedented accuracy. For example, Azevedo and Hoegner (2023) reveal that machine-learning-driven factor models can produce monthly returns surpassing traditional approaches, while Chen, Pelger, and Zhu (2024) demonstrate that deep neural networks yield superior Sharpe ratios and pricing precision.

AI also extends predictive power to volatility forecasting. Neural and convolutional networks outperform the heterogeneous autoregressive model in capturing nonlinear market dynamics (Christensen, Siggaard, and Veliyev 2023). Beyond equities, AI improves bond return prediction (Bianchi, Büchner, and Tamoni 2021) and foreign exchange modeling (Colombo, Forte, and Rossignoli 2019), enhancing global market efficiency.

Portfolio management, once dominated by the Markowitz mean-variance model, now benefits from machine learning's capacity to process massive datasets and dynamic inputs. Bradrania and Pirayesh Neghab (2022) and Aboussalah et al. (2024) integrate reinforcement learning and convolutional architectures into asset allocation, generating adaptive, robust portfolios that self-correct based on real-time market information.

AI also powers robo-advisors and automated trading. Uhl and Rohner (2018) document cost reductions up to 4.4% annually compared with human-managed portfolios. Meanwhile, Kaniel et al. (2023) show neural networks can identify outperforming mutual funds, while Manahov and Urquhart (2021) highlight AI's ability to model investor behavior in cryptocurrency markets.

Overall, these studies illustrate a paradigm shift from rule-based finance to data-driven, learning-based finance—where AI enables dynamic optimization, real-time prediction, and personalized investment strategies.

## Artificial Intelligence in Financial Markets and Institutions

### Bankruptcy Prediction and Fraud Detection

AI's predictive and pattern recognition capabilities have revolutionized risk management. Machine learning algorithms such as support vector machines, random forests, and Bayesian networks have surpassed traditional regression models in detecting early signs of financial distress or fraud. Mselmi, Lahiani, and Hamza (2017) achieved 94% accuracy in forecasting bankruptcies among French firms using hybrid support vector machines, while Cao et al.'s (2022) Bayesian model for firms in the United States achieved superior accuracy versus deep learning benchmarks.

In fraud detection, Bao et al. (2020) and Chen et al. (2017) demonstrated that raw financial and textual data analyzed by AI outperform ratio-based methods. NLP-powered systems can even detect narrative inconsistencies in annual reports, an innovation extended by Zhang and Liu (2024) to firms in the People's Republic of China using word embeddings, achieving 77% accuracy.

AI's real-time monitoring capabilities enable banks and regulators to identify anomalies and mitigate systemic risk. However, challenges persist, including class imbalance (with fraud cases being rare) and data manipulation through adversarial obfuscation.

### Sentiment Analysis

AI-driven sentiment analysis transforms how markets process unstructured data from news headlines to tweets. Early research from Antweiler and Frank (2004) relied on Naïve Bayes classifiers, but modern systems deploy long short-term memory networks, bidirectional encoder representations from transformers, and transformer architectures.

Empirical findings demonstrate significant predictive power: Bartov, Faurel, and Mohanram (2018) linked Twitter sentiment to firm-level earnings surprises; Ke, Kelly, and Xiu (2019) showed that machine-readable news signals improve return forecasts; and Cathcart et al. (2020) applied sentiment analytics to sovereign debt, linking news tone to credit spreads.

Crucially, Bertomeu et al. (2025) found that the "temporary ban of ChatGPT" in Italy reduced AI-related information efficiency—fewer analyst forecasts and slower market responses—highlighting how AI tools themselves shape capital market behavior.

### Consumer Risk and Financial Inclusion

AI-based credit scoring integrates alternative data such as mobile usage, e-commerce patterns, and transaction histories, enabling access to credit for previously unbanked populations (Björkegren and Grissen 2018). Random forests and deep learning methods outperform logistic models in predicting defaults (Butaru et al. 2016, Albanesi and Vamossy 2019).

However, algorithmic bias remains a pressing issue. Fuster et al. (2022) show that Black and Hispanic borrowers face disproportionately higher AI-driven loan rejections, while Dobbie et al. (2021) suggest that optimized models can still achieve fairness without sacrificing profitability.

These findings underscore AI's dual nature: It can enhance accuracy and inclusion or amplify social inequities depending on data governance and model transparency.

## Artificial Intelligence in Corporate Finance and Governance

### Corporate Outcomes and Performance

AI's applications extend to firm valuation, disclosure, and innovation. Babina et al. (2024) find that firms adopting AI report higher growth and innovation intensity. Research by Bao et al. (2020) and Brown, Crowley, and Elliott (2020) demonstrates that machine learning techniques can effectively detect earnings manipulation and linguistic obfuscation in financial reports. These methods are now gaining traction as tools for regulatory scrutiny.

AI also feeds back into corporate communication: As Cao et al. (2023) mentioned, companies increasingly tailor disclosures for algorithmic readers ("machine-friendly" filings), demonstrating how AI influences not only analysis but also corporate behavior itself.

### Executive and Governance Analytics

AI enables novel measurement of intangible managerial traits. NLP-based analyses of CEO letters and earnings calls reveal that managerial confidence and sentiment correlate with firm outcomes (Du et al. 2019). Computer vision further quantifies nonverbal cues: Dávila and Guasch (2022) found that body language affects valuation and investor perceptions.

These advancements contribute to "datafied governance," where machine learning quantifies leadership quality, culture, and risk-taking behavior (Li et al. 2021). AI thus becomes both a mirror and a metric for organizational behavior.

## Implications for Financial Stability

AI's integration into financial systems amplifies both efficiency and fragility. The reviewed literature identifies five interlinked risk dimensions: (i) systemic risk transmission, (ii) micro-prudential resilience, (iii) regulatory technology, (iv) market structure evolution, and (v) data-model-infrastructure dependence.

Specifically, our literature review devotes special attention to Asia's heterogeneous financial ecosystems, where AI-driven innovation coexists with uneven regulatory readiness. For instance, the People's Republic of China, with centralized data governance, leverages AI for real-time systemic monitoring but concentrates risk due to model homogenization—80% of bank risk models depend on dominant tech providers (Wang, Huang, and Hong 2024). In India, the integration of AI into its Unified Payments Interface reduces fraud by 50% yet exacerbates algorithmic exclusion, with rural borrowers facing 24% higher rejection rates (Anil and Misra 2022). Furthermore, Southeast Asian economies, particularly Malaysia and Indonesia, apply AI to Shariah-compliant finance and fintech inclusion, but they suffer from regulatory fragmentation and skill shortages (Arsyad, Kharisma, and Wiwoho 2025).

Ultimately, Asia must reconceptualize AI not merely as a regulatory target but as a co-evolutionary governance substrate to harness its benefits while containing continent-wide contagion risks.

## Conclusion

The literature reviewed paints a complex picture: AI is simultaneously a stabilizing intelligence and a source of adaptive fragility. On the one hand, it enhances efficiency, expands inclusion, and improves predictive precision across virtually every financial subfield. On the other hand, it concentrates power, embeds bias, and amplifies systemic linkages.

Given that AI's transformation of finance is already a reality, the critical task now is to adapt our governance frameworks. The goal is to steer this change toward outcomes that bolster financial stability and ensure equity.

The synthesis concludes that Asia, with its rapid digitalization and institutional diversity, is uniquely positioned to lead in AI governance innovation. If coordinated effectively, the region's experience could offer a global blueprint for balancing technological dynamism with systemic resilience.

## References

Aboussalah, A. M., X. Li, C. Chi, and R. Patel. 2024. The AI Black-Scholes: Finance-Informed Neural Network. arXiv preprint arXiv:2412.12213.

Albanesi, S., and D.F. Vamossy. 2019. Predicting Consumer Default: A Deep Learning Approach. *NBER Working Paper*. No. w26165. National Bureau of Economic Research.

Anil, K., and A. Misra. 2022. Artificial Intelligence in Peer-to-Peer Lending in India: A Cross-Case Analysis. *International Journal of Emerging Markets*. 17 (4). pp. 1085–1106.

Antweiler, W., and M. Z. Frank. 2004. Is All That Talk Just Noise? The Information Content of Internet Stock Message Boards. *The Journal of Finance*. 59 (3). pp. 1259–1294.

Arsyad, I., D. B. Kharisma, and J. Wiwoho. 2025. Artificial Intelligence and Islamic Finance Industry: Problems and Oversight. *International Journal of Law and Management*. https://doi.org/10.1108/ijlma-07-2024-0236.

Azevedo, V., and C. Hoegner. 2023. Enhancing Stock Market Anomalies with Machine Learning. *Review of Quantitative Finance and Accounting* 60 (1). pp. 195–230.

Babina, T., A. Fedyk, A. He, and J. Hodson. 2024. Artificial Intelligence, Firm Growth, and Product Innovation. *Journal of Financial Economics*. 151. 103745.

Bao, Y., B. Ke, Y. B. Li, Y. Julia, and J. Zhang. 2020. Detecting Accounting Fraud in Publicly Traded US Firms Using a Machine Learning Approach. *Journal of Accounting Research*. 58 (1). pp. 199–235.

Bartov, E., L. Faurel, and P. S. Mohanram. 2018. Can Twitter Help Predict Firm-Level Earnings and Stock Returns? *The Accounting Review*. 93 (3). pp. 25–57.

Bertomeu, J., Y. Lin, Y. Liu, and Z. Ni. 2025. The Impact of Generative AI on Information Processing: Evidence from the Ban of ChatGPT in Italy. *Journal of Accounting and Economics*. 101782.

Bianchi, D., M. Büchner, and A. Tamoni. 2021. Bond Risk Premiums with Machine Learning. *The Review of Financial Studies* 34 (2). pp. 1046–1089.

Björkegren, D., and D. Grissen. 2018. The Potential of Digital Credit to Bank the Poor. In *AEA Papers and Proceedings, Vol. 108*, pp. 68–71. Nashville: American Economic Association.

Bradrania, R., and D. Pirayesh Neghab. 2022. State-Dependent Asset Allocation Using Neural Networks. *The European Journal of Finance*. 28 (11). pp. 1130–1156.

Brown, N. C., R. M. Crowley, and W. B. Elliott. 2020. What Are You Saying? Using Topic to Detect Financial Misreporting. *Journal of Accounting Research* 58 (1). pp. 237–291.

Butaru, F., Q. Chen, B. Clark, S. Das, A. W. Lo, and A. Siddique. 2016. Risk and Risk Management in the Credit Card Industry. *Journal of Banking and Finance*. 72. 218–239.

Cao, Y., X. Liu, J. Zhai, and S. Hua. 2022. A Two-Stage Bayesian Network Model for Corporate Bankruptcy Prediction. *International Journal of Finance and Economics*. 27 (1). pp. 455–472.

Cao, S., W. Jiang, B. Yang, and A. L. Zhang. 2023. How To Talk When a Machine Is Listening: Corporate Disclosure in the Age of AI. *The Review of Financial Studies*. 36 (9): 3603–3642.

Cathcart, L., N. M. Gotthelf, M. Uhl, and Y. Shi. 2020. News Sentiment and Sovereign Credit Risk. *European Financial Management*. 26 (2). pp. 261–287.

Chen, L., M. Pelger, and J. Zhu. 2024. Deep Learning in Asset Pricing. *Management Science*. 70 (2). 714–750.

Chen, Y. J., C. H. Wu, Y. M. Chen, H. Y. Li, and H. K. Chen. 2017. Enhancement of Fraud Detection for Narratives in Annual Reports. *International Journal of Accounting Information Systems*. 26. pp. 32–45.

Christensen, K., M. Siggaard, and B. Veliyev. 2023. A Machine Learning Approach to Volatility Forecasting. *Journal of Financial Econometrics*. 21 (5). pp. 1680–1727.

Colombo, E., G. Forte, and R. Rossignoli. 2019. Carry Trade Returns with Support Vector Machines. *International Review of Finance*. 19 (3). pp. 483–504.

Dávila, A., and M. Guasch. 2022. Managers' Body Expansiveness, Investor Perceptions, and Firm Forecast Errors and Valuation. *Journal of Accounting Research*. 60 (2). pp. 517–563.

Dobbie, W., A. Liberman, D. Paravisini, and V. Pathania. 2021. Measuring Bias in Consumer Lending. *The Review of Economic Studies*. 88 (6). pp. 2799–2832.

Du, Q., Y. Jiao, P. Ye, and W. Fan. 2019. *When Mutual Fund Managers Write Confidently*. Available at SSRN 3513288.

Freyberger, J., A. Neuhierl, and M. Weber. 2020. Dissecting Characteristics Nonparametrically. *The Review of Financial Studies*. 33 (5). pp. 2326–2377.

Fuster, A., P. Goldsmith-Pinkham, T. Ramadorai, and A. Walther. 2022. Predictably Unequal? The Effects of Machine Learning on Credit Markets. *The Journal of Finance*. 77 (1). pp. 5–47.

Gu, S., B. Kelly, and D. Xiu. 2020. Empirical Asset Pricing via Machine Learning. *The Review of Financial Studies*. 33 (5). pp. 2223–2273.

Kaniel, R., Z. Lin, M. Pelger, and S. Van Nieuwerburgh. 2023. Machine-Learning the Skill of Mutual Fund Managers. *Journal of Financial Economics*. 150 (1). pp. 94–138.

Ke, Z. T., B. T. Kelly, and D. Xiu. 2019. Predicting Returns with Text Data. *NBER Working Paper*. No. w26186. National Bureau of Economic Research.

Li, K., F. Mai, R. Shen, and X. Yan. 2021. Measuring Corporate Culture Using Machine Learning. *The Review of Financial Studies*. 34 (7). pp. 3265–3315.

Manahov, V., and A. Urquhart. 2021. The Efficiency of Bitcoin: A Strongly Typed Genetic Programming Approach To Smart Electronic Bitcoin Markets. *International Review of Financial Analysis*. 73. 101629.

Mselmi, N., A. Lahiani, and T. Hamza. 2017. Financial Distress Prediction: The Case of French Small and Medium-Sized Firms. *International Review of Financial Analysis*. 50. pp. 67–80.

Uhl, M. W., and P. Rohner. 2018. Robo-Advisors versus Traditional Investment Advisors: An Unequal Game. *The Journal of Wealth Management*. 21 (1). 44–50.

Wang, L., Y. Huang, and Z. Hong. 2024. Digitalization as a Double-Edged Sword: A Deep Learning Analysis of Risk Management in Chinese Banks. *International Review of Financial Analysis*. 94.103249.

Zhang, T., and Z. Liu. 2024. Navigating Integration Through Rising Complexity: Convergence Dynamics in the ASEAN Banking Markets. *Open Economies Review*. 35 (4). 801–826.

# Mobilizing Capital for Local Government Finance in Asia and the Pacific Through GSS+ Bond Markets

## Urgent Need for Alternative Financing for Local Governments

Cities are central to economic activity and population growth, and they account for a large share of global energy use and greenhouse gas emissions. They comprise 56% of the world's population, generate over 80% of global gross domestic product, account for 70% of all energy use, and produce 75% of total greenhouse gas emissions.[17] They also face rising climate-related risks, creating substantial need for investments in mitigation, adaptation, and resilience.

Addressing these needs requires financing beyond central government budget allocations, making alternative capital sources essential for local governments to achieve their infrastructure and social development goals. In recent years, more local governments worldwide have tapped capital markets through the issuance of green, social, sustainability, and other labeled (GSS+) bonds to fund municipal infrastructure and meet their service delivery requirements. Economies such as Australia, Canada, Germany, India, Japan, the Netherlands, Norway, South Africa, Sweden, and Türkiye have effectively used these instruments and tapped into capital markets to deliver high-impact infrastructure projects and municipal services (**Figure 21**).

**Figure 21: Annual Issuance of Local Government Bonds Globally**

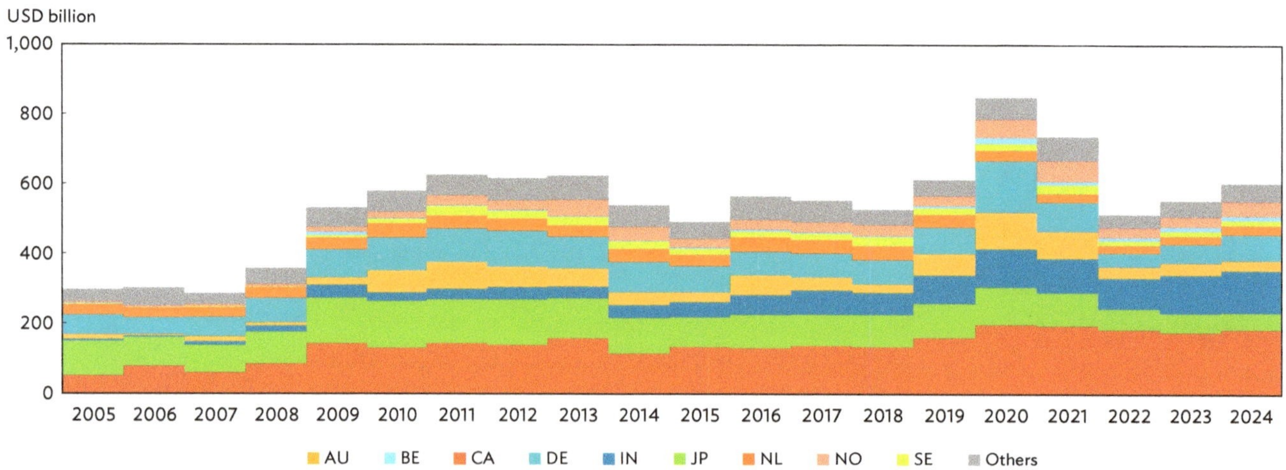


AU = Australia, BE = Belgium, CA = Canada, DE = Germany, IN = India, JP = Japan, NL = Netherlands, NO = Norway, SE = Sweden, USD = United States dollar.

Notes: Data as of 31 March 2025. Issuance amounts are based on USD equivalent values at the time of issuance. Municipal bond market issuance tends to increase during times of crisis such as the global financial crisis and the coronavirus disease (COVID-19) pandemic.

Source: Authors' calculations based on Bloomberg LP data

This special section was written by Kosintr Puongsophol (senior financial sector specialist) and Pitchaya Sirivunnabood (consultant) at the Asian Development Bank. For more information on this topic, please visit https://www.adb.org/publications/capital-local-government-finance-asia-pacific.

17 World Bank. 2023. Development Topics—Urban Development Overview. https://www.worldbank.org/en/topic/urbandevelopment/overview; International Energy Agency. 2024. Executive Summary to *Empowering Urban Energy Transitions*. https://www.iea.org/reports/empowering-urban-energy-transitions/executive-summary.

## Why GSS+ Bonds Matter and What They Can Finance

GSS+ bonds are not only an alternative financing source for local governments but also a strategic tool that can encourage local governments to develop climate-resilient infrastructure, strengthen their ability to manage and withstand climate-related risks, and provide essential social services to local communities. These instruments help create investment opportunities that deepen citizen engagement by fostering a sense of ownership in local development initiatives. In addition, GSS+ bonds contribute to the development of local capital markets by providing long-term, competitively priced instruments for local investors and by attracting a broad base of investors seeking sustainable finance opportunities.

In principle, GSS+ bonds are designed to finance green and social projects—including those focused on mitigation, adaptation, and resilience—which aligns with local government's responsibilities in delivering infrastructure and meeting social needs. Examples of eligible bond-financed projects—based on their use-of-proceeds requirements—that are most relevant to local governments are shown in **Table 2**.

**Table 2: Examples of Eligible Projects**

| Mitigation | Adaptation and Resilience |
|---|---|
| • Sustainable water and sewer infrastructure<br>• Clean mass transit<br>• Clean energy installation and generation promotion<br>• Green public buildings<br>• Energy efficiency retrofitting for municipal facilities<br>• Local environmental preservation (e.g., parks and green space development) | • Infrastructure for flood and stormwater management (e.g., levees, seawalls, and permeable pavements)<br>• Measures for drought and water stress resilience (e.g., waterworks efficiency, and leak detection and management)<br>• Measures for heat-resilience (e.g., urban cooling centers and green corridors)<br>• Climate-smart public buildings (e.g., flood-proofing and elevated public buildings)<br>• Nature-based solutions (e.g., wetland and mangrove restoration and shoreline stabilization) |
| **Social** | |
| • Access to essential services (e.g., education, health, and social inclusion)<br>• Affordable housing, healthcare, and education<br>• Affordable basic infrastructure (e.g., development of transport, energy, and green spaces)<br>• Employment creation and SME financing | |

SME = small and medium-sized enterprise.

Source: ADB. 2025. *Mobilizing Capital for Local Government Finance in Asia and the Pacific through Green, Social, and Sustainability Bond Markets.* https://www.adb.org/sites/default/files/publication/1108181/capital-local-government-finance-asia-pacific.pdf.

To issue GSS+ municipal bonds, local governments need to develop sustainable financing frameworks that can be tailored for their strategic priorities and unique municipal or regional situations. It also requires local governments to establish effective impact data tracking and reporting systems to enhance their ability to develop and identify a pipeline of eligible investment projects with clear repayment sources—all of which can help build investor confidence.

## Key Recommendations

Mobilizing capital through GSS+ bond issuance can be an effective instrument for local governments to mobilize sustainable finance for projects that deliver positive economic, environmental, and social benefits. Several practical, market-based steps can support this approach:

- **Align local government project financing with sovereign sustainability financing frameworks.** Central governments can advance domestic development priorities by enabling responsible municipal borrowing that addresses sustainability challenges at the local level. Local governments can align their sustainability financing frameworks with those of the central government to ensure policy coherence; enhance credibility with investors; and facilitate access to capital markets by leveraging established domestic standards, taxonomies, and reporting systems.
- **Strengthen fiscal oversight, disclosure, and governance frameworks for sustainable local government financing.** This includes frameworks based on green and social taxonomies. Demonstrating institutional integrity and capacity for responsible fundraising through robust financial and sustainability disclosure and high-quality governance frameworks boosts investor confidence and supports sustainable access to capital markets, in addition to fostering a secure and reliable repayment structure of local-government-financed projects.
- **Establish pooled local government financing vehicles to scale up local government bond markets, with a focus on green and social finance.** Pooled financing vehicles aggregate local issuance needs and consolidate resources into a single well-capitalized entity. While this model offers the advantages of lower borrowing

costs, improved operational efficiency, enhanced market credibility, and increased transparency and functionality of municipal finance markets, it comes with more legal and institutional complexity. It also requires robust governance frameworks and clear institutional arrangements among participating local governments.

- **Leverage multinational development bank resources and guarantees to kickstart local government bond markets.** Development finance organizations can play a catalytic role in developing municipal finance markets through both financial support and technical assistance. Examples of such support include initial capital contributions, partial credit guarantees, and technical assistance for developing subnational borrowing frameworks and preparing project pipelines. For example, Asian Development Bank's GSS+ Bonds Initiative offers advisory support to catalyze signature GSS+ bond issuance and create environments for growth across Southeast Asia.

# Market Summaries

## People's Republic of China

### Yield Movements

**The local currency (LCY) government bond yield curve of the People's Republic of China (PRC) steepened between 3 November and 6 February on falling yields.** Yields fell for most tenors in the PRC over weak inflation data and increased liquidity from the central bank (**Figure 1**). Yields fell an average of 4 basis points (bps) for the 8-year tenor and below, excluding the 3-month and 5-year tenors. Meanwhile, yields for the 10-year and the 30-year tenors remained elevated during the review period as steep declines in January and February failed to fully offset previous increases. The PRC's yields rose mostly from the end of December through the first week of January over expectations of increasing inflation amid a positive growth outlook, which was also reflected in stock market gains at that time, reversing previous negative sentiment. Consumer price inflation rose strongly to 0.8% year-on-year (y-o-y) in December and 0.7% y-o-y in November from 0.2% y-o-y in October. Yields subsequently declined for the remainder of the review period on several factors. Consumer price inflation fell to 0.2% y-o-y in January. In addition, the PRC's efforts to slow the stock market's appreciation caused the return of some funds to the bond market. Lastly, the People's Bank of China added liquidity to financial markets via reverse repos and medium-term lending.

**Figure 1: The People's Republic of China's Benchmark Yield Curve—Local Currency Government Bonds**

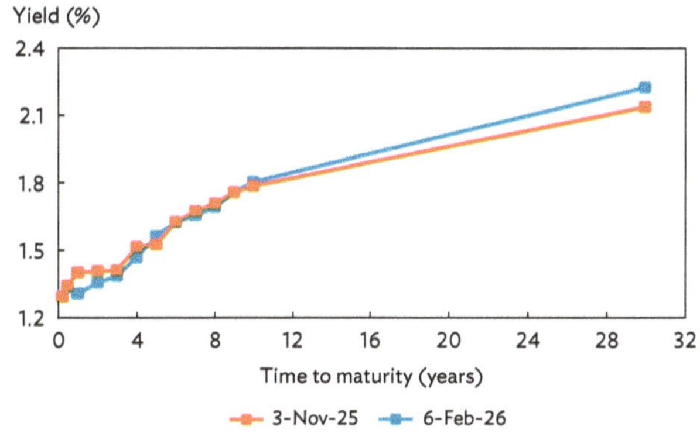


Source: Based on data from Bloomberg LP.

### Local Currency Bond Market Size and Issuance

**The PRC's bond market expansion decelerated slightly in Q4 2025, with the stock of outstanding bonds reaching CNY174.7 trillion, as the government had already completed most of its funding in previous quarters.** The LCY bond market's expansion moderated to 2.2% quarter-on-quarter (q-o-q) in the fourth quarter (Q4) of 2025 from 3.4% q-o-q in the previous quarter (**Figure 2**). Slower gains were seen mostly in the government bond market over a decline in financing activity as the end of the year approached. In particular, policy bank bonds outstanding were mostly unchanged at the end of December from the previous quarter, while both Treasury bonds and local government bonds posted slower growth rates. Meanwhile, corporate bonds outstanding maintained their rate of increase as fewer bonds matured in the quarter.

**Figure 2: Composition of Local Currency Bonds Outstanding in the People's Republic of China**

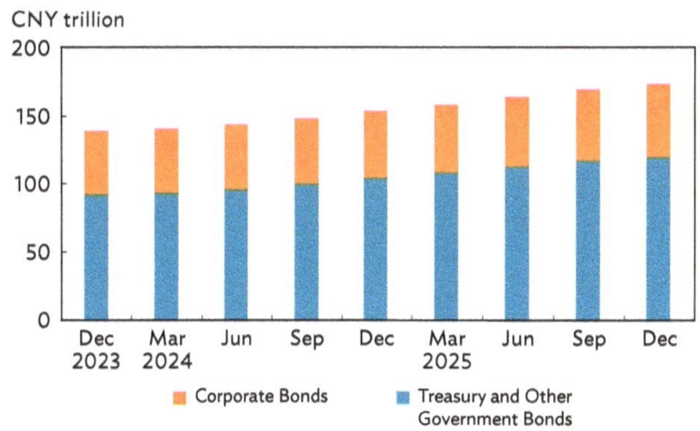


CNY = Chinese yuan.
Source: CEIC Data Company.

This market summary was written by Russ Jason Lo (consultant) in the Economic Research and Development Impact Department, Asian Development Bank, Manila.

**The PRC saw reduced bond issuance in Q4 2025 in both the government and corporate sectors.** The largest decline was seen in government issuance, which fell 22.6% q-o-q (**Figure 3**). Issuance contracted the most for local government bonds (–42.3%) and policy bank bonds (–42.2%). Policy bank bond issuance declined as there had been accelerated issuance in the previous quarter to avoid the pending imposition of value-added taxes. Corporate bond issuance contracted 5.4% q-o-q over uncertainty in the PRC's economy.

**Figure 3: Composition of Local Currency Bond Issuance in the People's Republic of China**

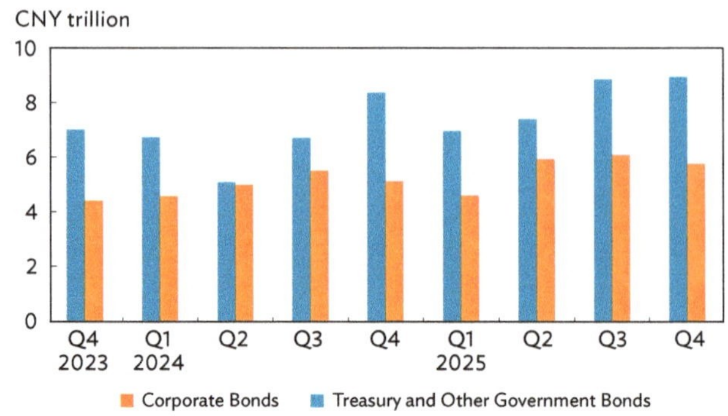


CNY = Chinese yuan, Q1 = first quarter, Q2 = second quarter, Q3 = third quarter, Q4 = fourth quarter.

Source: CEIC Data Company.

## Investor Profile

**Banks continued to purchase Treasury bonds amid increased liquidity as well as a slowdown in loan growth.** Banks added significantly more Treasury bonds at the end of 2025, with the share of total Treasury bond holdings rising to 69.2% from 66.6% in the previous year. The move came following announcement that the People's Bank of China had resumed bond buying in October and indications that it would support liquidity. Bond demand was also fueled by weak loan growth, as banks needed to reinvest their customer deposits. In contrast, the share of unincorporated products, which are bank products offered to retail clients such as wealth management products, fell to 7.7% at the end of 2025 from 8.3% a year earlier as retail investors allocated more to equities.

**Figure 4: Investor Profile of Treasury Bonds**

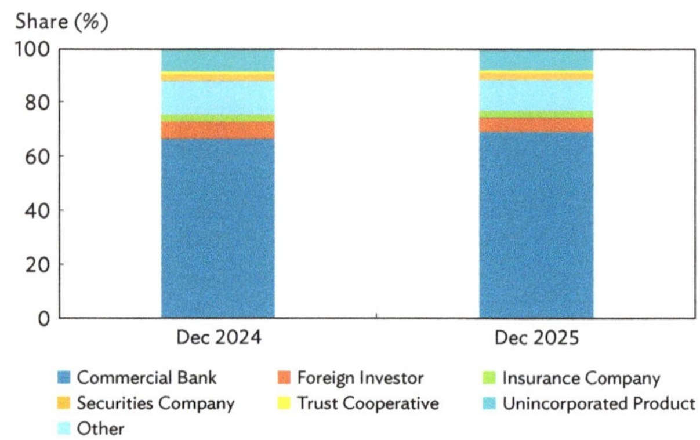


Source: CEIC Data Company.

## Sustainable Bond Market

**Sustainable bonds outstanding in the PRC continued to expand in 2025 on robust issuance.** The PRC's sustainable bond market reached a size of USD409.4 billion at the end of 2025, representing 53.5% of emerging East Asia's sustainable bond total.[18] The rate of market expansion ticked up to 10.5% y-o-y in 2025 from 6.8% y-o-y in 2024, supported by strong issuance of USD147.8 billion, which comprised 64.0% of the regional total. The PRC's outstanding sustainable bonds were predominantly green bonds, which accounted for 85.8% of the market's total. The issuance surge in 2025 was driven by the PRC's need to meet the goals stated in the 14th Five-Year Plan for a Modern Energy System, which required the PRC to attain certain green energy milestones by the end of 2025. The next largest share was for sustainability bonds, which comprised 8.4% of the PRC's sustainable bonds outstanding.

**Figure 5: Sustainable Bonds Outstanding in the People's Republic of China**

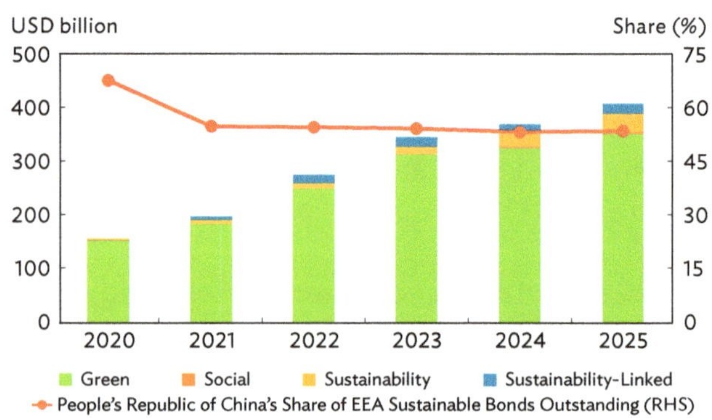


EEA = emerging East Asia, RHS = right-hand side, USD = United States dollar.

Notes:

1. Emerging East Asia is defined to include the member states of ASEAN plus the People's Republic of China; Hong Kong, China; and the Republic of Korea.
2. Data include both local currency and foreign currency sustainable bonds.
3. Sustainability-linked bonds include transition-linked bonds.

Source: *AsianBondsOnline* calculations based on Bloomberg LP data.

[18] Emerging East Asia is defined to include member states of the Association of Southeast Asian Nations plus the People's Republic of China; Hong Kong, China; and the Republic of Korea.

# Hong Kong, China

## Yield Movements

**Between 3 November and 6 February, the yield curve for local currency (LCY) government bonds in Hong Kong, China steepened.** Yields fell an average of 63 basis points (bps) for bonds with maturities of up to 3 years but edged up an average of 12 bps for bonds with maturities of 10 years and longer (**Figure 1**). The yield spread between 2- and 10-year bonds widened to 89 bps from 44 bps during the review period. Yields at the shorter end of the curve declined after the 25 bps downward adjustment of the base rate by the Hong Kong Monetary Authority on 11 December, following the United States Federal Reserve's 25 bps rate cut. The rate adjustment lowered borrowing costs, including bond yields. Meanwhile, yields rose for longer-term bonds on increased supply with the reopening of 10-year and 15-year Hong Kong Special Administrative Region (HKSAR) government infrastructure bonds during the review period. The steepening of the yield curve also reflected market expectations of faster economic growth. Hong Kong, China's year-on-year (y-o-y) economic expansion quickened to 3.8% in the fourth quarter (Q4) of 2025 from 3.7% in the previous quarter, propelled by faster growth in exports, particularly electronics, and private consumption.

**Figure 1: Hong Kong, China's Benchmark Yield Curve—Local Currency Government Bonds**

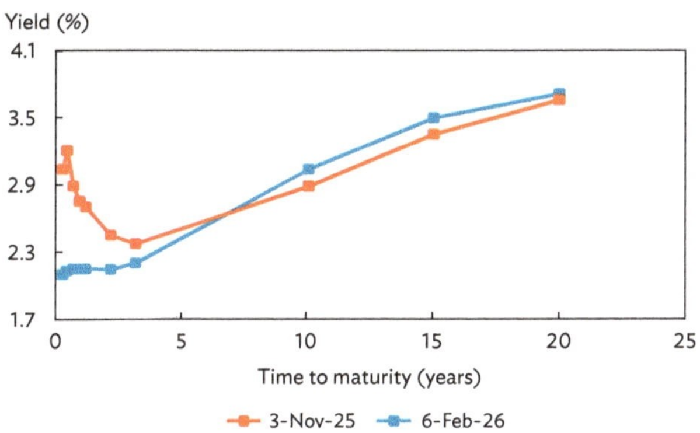


Source: Based on data from Bloomberg LP.

## Local Currency Bond Market Size and Issuance

**Hong Kong, China's LCY bond market expanded faster in Q4 2025, supported by a high volume of government bond issuance.** LCY bonds outstanding reached HKD3,679.7 billion at the end of December, with growth accelerating to 6.3% quarter-on-quarter (q-o-q) from 4.7% q-o-q in the previous quarter (**Figure 2**). This faster expansion was underpinned by a rebound in the HKSAR government bond stock—which surged 24.4% q-o-q to HKD320.1 billion in Q4 2025 after contracting in the prior quarter—on robust issuance, including HKD55.0 billion worth of Silver Bonds.[19] Corporate bonds outstanding (HKD2,017.6 billion) continued to expand in Q4 2025, although growth decelerated to 7.8% q-o-q from 11.1% q-o-q in the prior quarter as a slowdown in issuance and a larger volume of maturities capped growth.

**Figure 2: Composition of Local Currency Bonds Outstanding in Hong Kong, China**

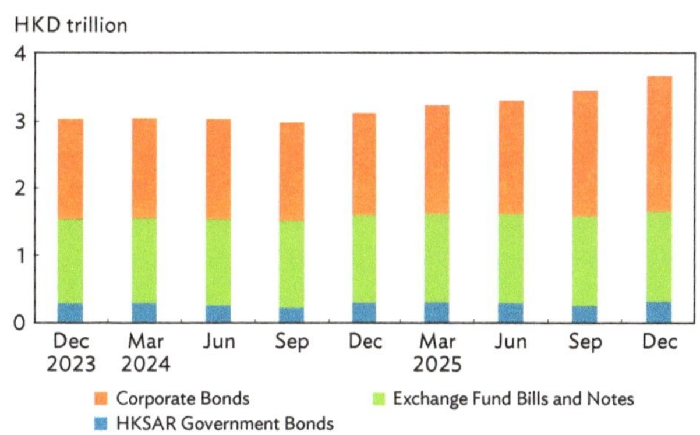


HKD = Hong Kong dollar, HKSAR = Hong Kong Special Administrative Region.
Source: Hong Kong Monetary Authority.

This market summary was written by Debbie Gundaya (consultant) in the Economic Research and Development Impact Department, Asian Development Bank, Manila.

19 Silver Bonds are 3-year retail government bonds specifically offered to senior citizens in Hong Kong, China.

**LCY bond issuance growth moderated in Q4 2025 on lower debt sales from the private sector.** New issues of LCY bonds grew 4.0% q-o-q to HKD1,643.7 billion, which was slower than the 9.2% q-o-q growth in the previous quarter (**Figure 3**). Corporate bond sales fell 17.7% q-o-q to HKD410.8 billion, dragged down by subdued issuance from real estate firms. Meanwhile, issuance of HKSAR government bonds jumped nearly ninefold to HKD64.8 billion, driven largely by a HKD55.0 billion issuance of Silver Bonds in October. Other government issuances during the quarter included reopenings of infrastructure bonds with maturities of 3–15 years totaling HKD5.8 billion, HKD2.5 billion of 2-year digital green bonds, and HKD1.5 billion of 1-year floating-rate notes.[20]

**Figure 3: Composition of Local Currency Bond Issuance in Hong Kong, China**

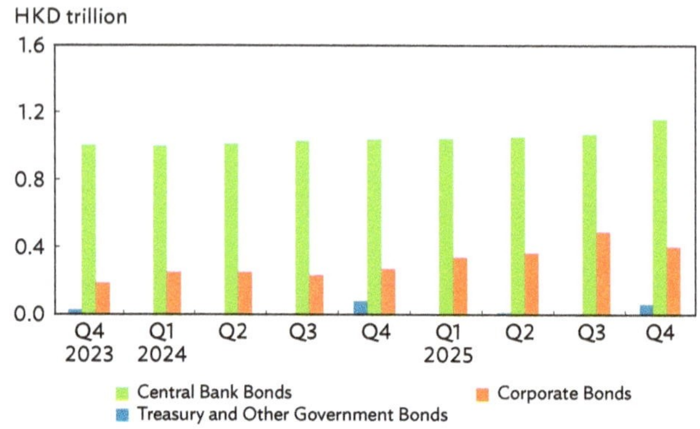


HKD = Hong Kong dollar, Q1 = first quarter, Q2 = second quarter, Q3 = third quarter, Q4 = fourth quarter.
Source: Hong Kong Monetary Authority.

## Sustainable Bond Market

**Sustained public sector issuance continued to spur Hong Kong, China's sustainable bond market in 2025.** The stock of sustainable bonds has increased over fivefold since 2020, reaching USD46.6 billion at the end of 2025 and comprising 6.1% of the emerging East Asian total (**Figure 4**).[21] Total sustainable bonds outstanding saw a decline of 3.1% y-o-y in 2025, reversing robust 10.3% y-o-y growth in 2024, as heightened global uncertainty dampened investor sentiment and capped private sector issuance in 2025. Private sector issuances tallied USD2.2 billion in 2025, down 61.3% from USD5.7 billion in the previous year. The largest corporate issuer in 2025 was CCB Shipping and Leasing, with USD800.0 million of green bonds, followed by Swire Properties, with total issuance worth USD526.5 million of green bonds denominated in Hong Kong dollars and Chinese yuan. Meanwhile, public sector issuances grew 2.0% y-o-y to USD4.0 billion in 2025. In June, the Government of the Hong Kong Special Administrative Region of the People's Republic of China issued a multicurrency tranche of green bonds worth a total of USD2.7 billion. This was followed by a multicurrency digital green bond offering in November worth the equivalent of USD1.3 billion and denominated in Hong Kong dollars, Chinese yuan, euros, and United States dollars. It was Hong Kong, China's third issuance of tokenized green bonds as part of initiatives to promote fintech and develop its sustainable bond market.

**Figure 4: Sustainable Bonds Outstanding in Hong Kong, China**

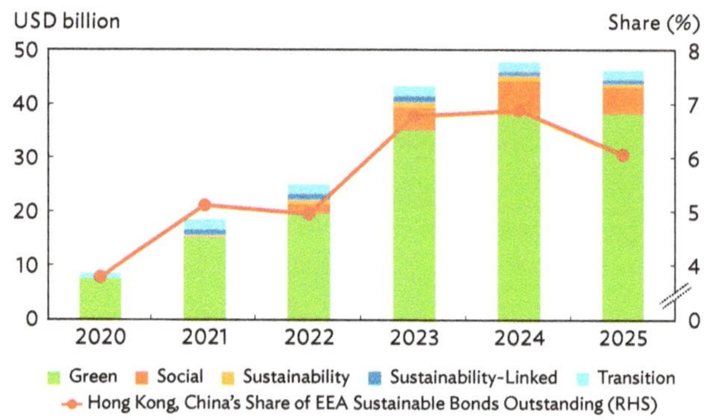


EEA = emerging East Asia, RHS = right-hand side, USD = United States dollar.
Notes:
1. Emerging East Asia is defined to include the member states of ASEAN plus the People's Republic of China; Hong Kong, China; and the Republic of Korea.
2. Data include both local currency and foreign currency sustainable bonds.
3. Sustainability-linked bonds include transition-linked bonds.

Source: *AsianBondsOnline* calculations based on Bloomberg LP data.

[20] The 2-year green bonds were part of a multicurrency digital green bond issuance under the HKSAR Government Sustainable Bond Programme.

[21] Emerging East Asia is defined to include member states of the Association of Southeast Asian Nations plus the People's Republic of China; Hong Kong, China; and the Republic of Korea.

# Indonesia

## Yield Movements

**Indonesia's local currency (LCY) government bond yields collectively rose between 3 November and 6 February, rising an average of 19 basis points across the curve (Figure 1).** Yields gained as investor sentiment was dampened over an equities market rout that occurred in January in response to MSCI warnings about a potential reduction in Indonesia's stock weighting in the MSCI Emerging Market Index or even a possible downgrade of Indonesia's stock market classification to the Frontier Market Index. In addition, concerns over the government's fiscal policy contributed to the negative sentiment as 2025's budget deficit (2.9% of gross domestic product) nearly breached the 3.0% statutory debt limit. Yields rose further after Moody's downgraded Indonesia's sovereign credit rating outlook from Stable to Negative on 5 February. Meanwhile, Bank Indonesia continued to maintain an accommodative monetary stance, having left the policy rate unchanged at 4.75% since September.

**Figure 1: Indonesia's Benchmark Yield Curve—Local Currency Government Bonds**

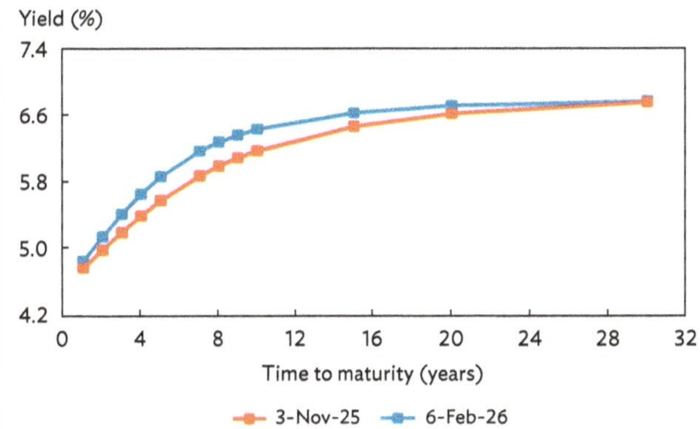


Source: Based on data from Bloomberg LP.

## Local Currency Bond Market Size and Issuance

**The expansion of Indonesia's LCY bond market accelerated slightly in the fourth quarter (Q4) of 2025, buoyed by both the government and corporate bond segments.** By the end of 2025, the outstanding size of Indonesia's LCY bond market reached IDR8,067.1 trillion, with the expansion inching up to 1.6% quarter-on-quarter (q-o-q) in Q4 2025 from 1.4% q-o-q in the third quarter (**Figure 2**). Despite a slowdown in issuance, corporate bonds outstanding gained 3.9% q-o-q in Q4 2025, up from 3.7% q-o-q in the previous quarter, due to a reduced volume of maturities. Meanwhile, the government bond market's expansion moderated to 1.7% q-o-q from 2.4% q-o-q due to the front-loading of issuance in prior quarters.

**Figure 2: Composition of Local Currency Bonds Outstanding in Indonesia**

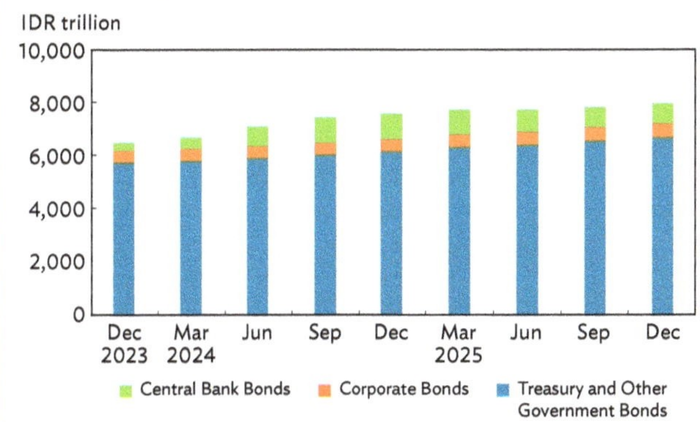


IDR = Indonesian rupiah.

Sources: Bank Indonesia; Directorate General of Budget Financing and Risk Management, Ministry of Finance; and Indonesia Stock Exchange.

**LCY bond issuance marginally contracted in Q4 2025 over reduced government and corporate bond issuance.** Total LCY bond issuance fell to IDR921.7 trillion in Q4 2025 on a marginal decline of 0.1% q-o-q (**Figure 3**). Government bond issuance contracted 24.3% q-o-q as the government had mostly fulfilled its annual borrowing in the prior quarters. Corporate bond issuance fell 13.9% q-o-q due to a high base effect resulting from increased third quarter issuance driven by lower borrowing costs following policy rate cuts by Bank Indonesia. The largest corporate bond issuance in Q4 2025 was from state-owned Sarana Multi Infrastruktur, which sold multitranche bonds amounting to IDR6.5 trillion, comprising 11.1% of Indonesia's corporate bond issuance total during the quarter.

This market summary was written by Roselyn Regalado (consultant) in the Economic Research and Development Impact Department, Asian Development Bank, Manila.

**Figure 3: Composition of Local Currency Bond Issuance in Indonesia**

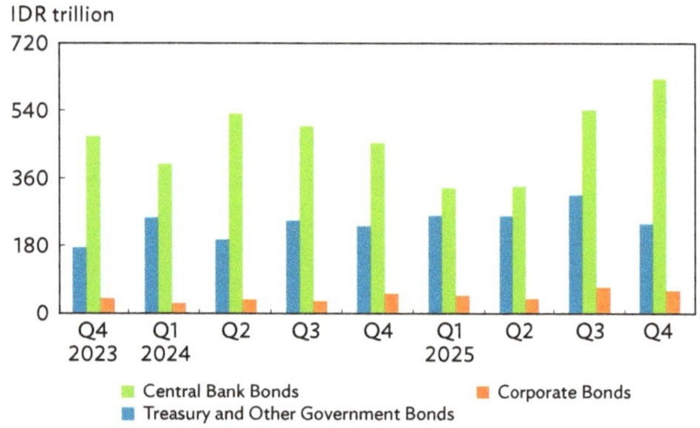


IDR = Indonesian rupiah, Q1 = first quarter, Q2 = second quarter, Q3 = third quarter, Q4 = fourth quarter.

Sources: Bank Indonesia; Directorate General of Budget Financing and Risk Management, Ministry of Finance; and Indonesia Stock Exchange.

**Figure 4: Investor Profile of Tradable Government Bonds**

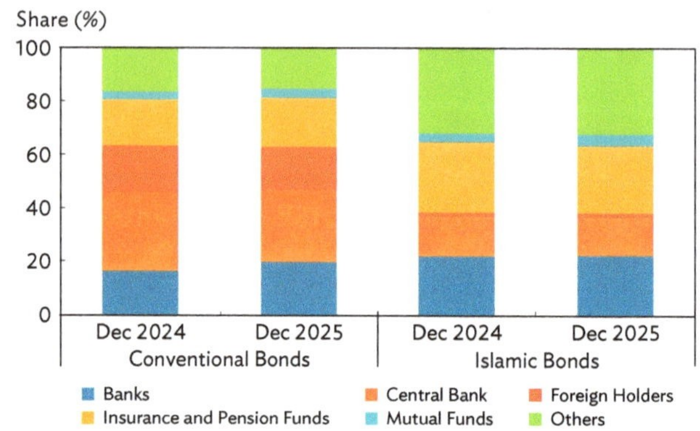


Source: Directorate General of Budget Financing and Risk Management, Ministry of Finance.

## Investor Profile

**The central bank remained the largest holder of Treasury bonds in Indonesia at the end of 2025.** However, the central bank's holdings share slightly dipped to 25.0% at the end of 2025 from 26.8% a year earlier. By instrument type, Bank Indonesia held 27.3% of conventional bonds and 14.3% of outstanding *sukuk* (Islamic bonds) at the end of 2025 (**Figure 4**). Foreign investors reduced their holdings of Treasury bonds to 13.4% in 2025 from 14.5% in 2024 as investor sentiment soured over concerns about the government's fiscal policy. Meanwhile, domestic financial institutions continued to buy Treasury bonds, with banks increasing their holdings share to 20.2% from 17.4%.

## Sustainable Bond Market

**Sustainable bonds outstanding in Indonesia expanded 23.7% year-on-year (y-o-y) in 2025, up from a 17.4% y-o-y gain in 2024, to reach USD17.5 billion at the end of December.** The expansion lifted Indonesia's share of emerging East Asia's sustainable bond total to 2.3% in 2025 from 2.0% a year earlier (**Figure 5**).[22] Favorable financial conditions bolstered issuance during the year, with issuance rising 34.5% y-o-y to USD4.5 billion. Of this amount, 67.1% came from the Government of Indonesia, the largest of which was the USD1.1 billion green *sukuk* issued in July and the EUR0.6 billion sovereign sustainability bond issued in October. The active participation of the public sector in the sustainable bond market contributed to the lengthening of the maturity structure. Public sector sustainable bonds carried longer tenors than their private sector counterparts, with 62.9% having tenors of over 5 years, which resulted in an average size-weighted tenor of 8.6 years at the end of 2025. For private sector sustainable bonds, tenors of 5 years or less comprised 70.3% of the total, generating a size-weighted average tenor of 4.4 years.

**Figure 5: Sustainable Bonds Outstanding in Indonesia**

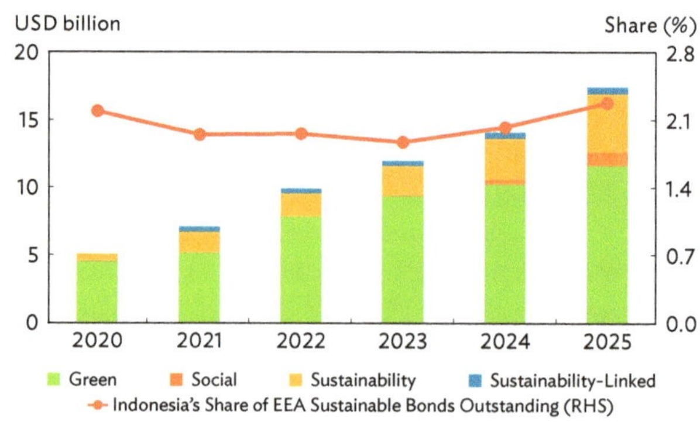


EEA = emerging East Asia, RHS = right-hand side, USD = United States dollar.

Notes:

1. Emerging East Asia is defined to include the member states of ASEAN plus the People's Republic of China; Hong Kong, China; and the Republic of Korea.
2. Data include both local currency and foreign currency sustainable bonds.
3. Sustainability-linked bonds include transition-linked bonds.

Source: *AsianBondsOnline* calculations based on Bloomberg LP data.

[22] Emerging East Asia is defined to include member states of the Association of Southeast Asian Nations plus the People's Republic of China; Hong Kong, China; and the Republic of Korea.

# Republic of Korea

## Yield Movements

**The Republic of Korea's local currency (LCY) government bond yield curve shifted upward between 3 November and 6 February as the Bank of Korea (BOK) pursued a hawkish policy stance.** Yields rose an average of 43 basis points for all tenors following the BOK's 15 January monetary policy meeting statement signaling the possible end of its easing cycle (**Figure 1**). The BOK maintained the base rate at 2.50% at both its 27 November and 15 January meetings amid stable economic growth and inflation, and as risks to financial stability remained. Risks continued to include rising household debt and housing prices, and foreign exchange volatility. The BOK also removed language on any "further potential rate cuts," which had appeared in previous statements, from its January monetary policy statement. In addition, the number of members open to a rate cut within the next 3 months declined to one from three (out of six) in the November meeting, increasing the possibility of there being no rate cut in the near term. Subsequently, the BOK held the base rate unchanged at 2.50% in its 26 February meeting.

**Figure 1: The Republic of Korea's Benchmark Yield Curve—Local Currency Government Bonds**

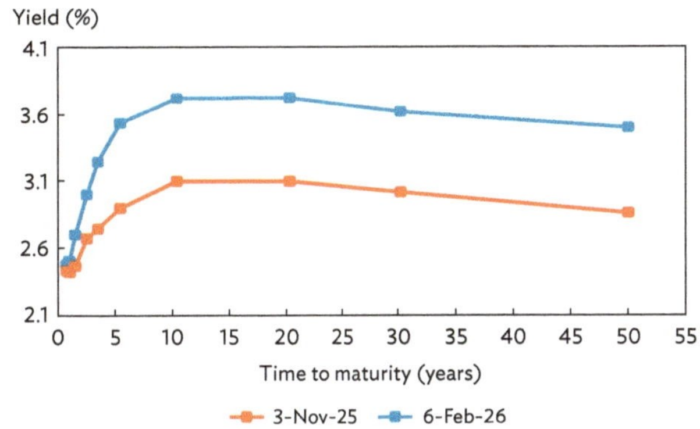


Source: Based on data from Bloomberg LP.

## Local Currency Bond Market Size and Issuance

**Expansion of the Republic of Korea's LCY bonds outstanding eased in the fourth quarter (Q4) of 2025 on reduced issuance of government bonds.** Total LCY bonds outstanding in the Republic of Korea reached KRW3,496.1 trillion at the end of December, reflecting an increase of 1.4% quarter-on-quarter (q-o-q) (**Figure 2**). The expansion moderated from 2.3% q-o-q in the third quarter (Q3) of 2025 due to reduced issuance of government bonds. Government bonds outstanding marginally increased 0.6% q-o-q, while expansion in the corporate bond segment was roughly stable at 1.9% q-o-q in Q4 2025.

**Figure 2: Composition of Local Currency Bonds Outstanding in the Republic of Korea**

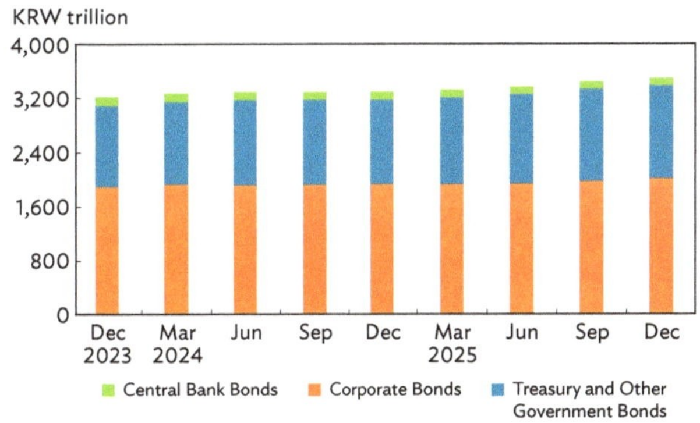


KRW = Korean won.

Sources: Bank of Korea and KG Zeroin Corp.

**LCY bond issuance in the Republic of Korea rose in Q4 2025, solely driven by the corporate bond segment.** Total LCY bond issuance grew 3.4% q-o-q in Q4 2025, accelerating from a 2.8% q-o-q increase in Q3 2025, as the quarterly surge in corporate bond issuance outpaced the contraction in government bonds (**Figure 3**). Issuance of government bonds fell 30.4% q-o-q as the government had met most of its funding needs in prior quarters. Corporate bond sales surged 21.0% q-o-q, largely driven by the finance sector. Banks increased their issuance of bonds in Q4 2025 to secure liquidity amid an outflow of funds from low-yield bank deposits as investors sought higher returns in the equity market.

This market summary was written by Angelica Andrea Cruz (consultant) in the Economic Research and Development Impact Department, Asian Development Bank, Manila.

**Figure 3: Composition of Local Currency Bond Issuance in the Republic of Korea**

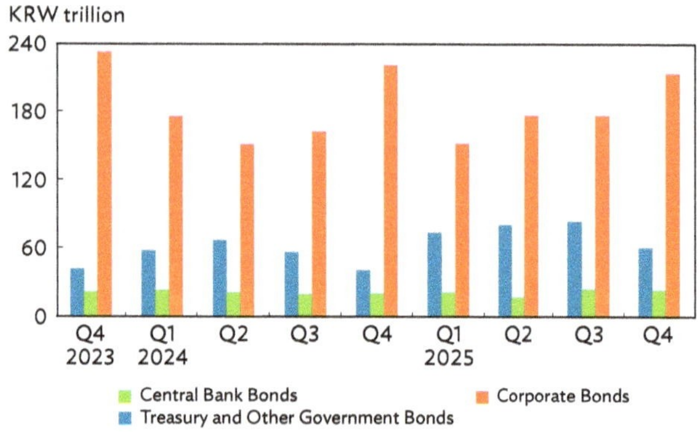


KRW = Korean won, Q1 = first quarter, Q2 = second quarter, Q3 = third quarter, Q4 = fourth quarter.

Sources: Bank of Korea and KG Zeroin Corp.

**Figure 4: Local Currency Bonds Outstanding Investor Profile**

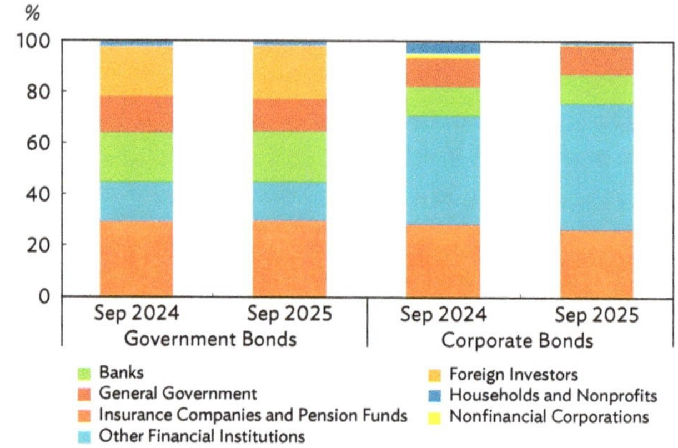


Sources: *AsianBondsOnline* and Bank of Korea.

## Investor Profile

**The Republic of Korea's LCY government bond segment has a more diverse investor profile than the corporate bond segment.** LCY government bonds outstanding continued to be held by five major investor groups—led by insurance companies and foreign investors with shares of 30.4% and 21.0%, respectively, at the end of September 2025 (**Figure 4**). Other major investor groups and their respective holdings share include banks (19.6%), other financial institutions (15.2%), and the general government (12.6%). Meanwhile, the LCY corporate bond market's investor profile comprises two major groups. Other financial institutions held almost half of corporate bonds outstanding at the end of 2025, with their collective share increasing to 49.5% from 42.7% a year earlier, followed by insurance companies with a share of 27.0%, down from 29.0%.

## Sustainable Bond Market

**The Republic of Korea's sustainable bond market reached a size of USD188.4 billion at the end of 2025, remaining the second-largest sustainable bond market in emerging East Asia.**[23] The Republic of Korea's sustainable bonds outstanding comprised 24.6% of the regional total. While its share of the regional total has declined in recent years, the Republic of Korea's sustainable bond market continued to grow in 2025, albeit at a slower pace following rapid expansion during the COVID-19 pandemic (**Figure 5**). Total sustainable bonds outstanding rose 2.3% year-on-year (y-o-y) in 2025, moderating from 4.0% y-o-y in 2024, as issuance marginally declined 1.9% y-o-y. By bond type, social bonds continued to dominate the Republic of Korea's sustainable bond market with a share of 53.6%. Most social bonds come from the public sector, led by Korea Housing Finance, which provides sustainable housing finance. Green bonds comprise the second-largest share at 28.9%, primarily comprising issuances from the private sector. Around 70% of total sustainable bonds outstanding have remaining maturities of less than 3 years, resulting in a size-weighted average tenor of 2.9 years.

**Figure 5: Sustainable Bonds Outstanding in the Republic of Korea**

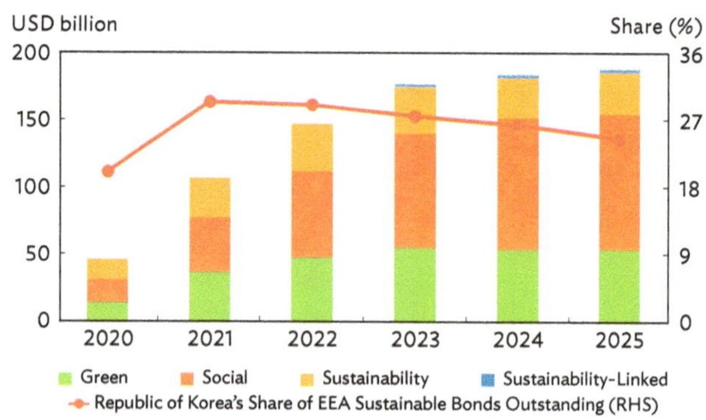


EEA = emerging East Asia, RHS = right-hand side, USD = United States dollar.

Notes:

1. Emerging East Asia is defined to include the member states of ASEAN plus the People's Republic of China; Hong Kong, China; and the Republic of Korea.
2. Data include both local currency and foreign currency sustainable bonds.
3. Sustainability-linked bonds include transition-linked bonds.

Source: *AsianBondsOnline* calculations based on Bloomberg LP data.

[23] Emerging East Asia is defined to include member states of the Association of Southeast Asian Nations plus the People's Republic of China; Hong Kong, China; and the Republic of Korea.

# Malaysia

## Yield Movements

**Figure 1: Malaysia's Benchmark Yield Curve—Local Currency Government Bonds**

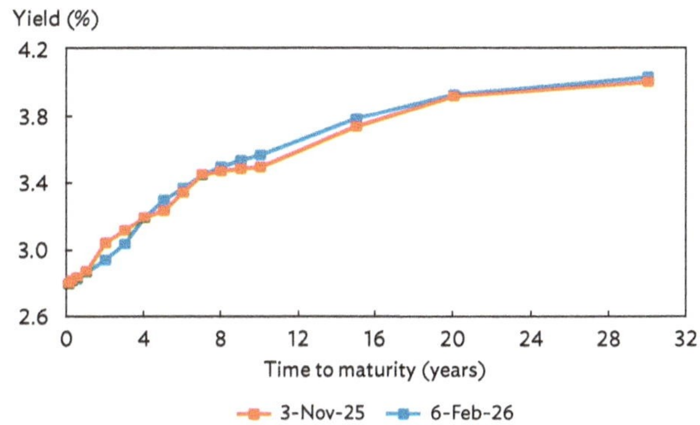


Source: Based on data from Bloomberg LP.

**Malaysia's yield curve slightly steepened between 3 November and 6 February.** Bond yields declined an average of 3 basis points (bps) for maturities of 4 years or less, with the 2-year and 3-year bonds posting the largest declines of 10 bps and 8 bps, respectively (**Figure 1**). Yields declined amid improved sentiment as the government aims to reduce the budget deficit in 2026 to 3.5% of gross domestic product from 3.7% in 2025. The improved fiscal outlook spurred investor interest, with foreign inflows skewed toward the front end of the yield curve, exerting downward pressure on shorter-dated yields. Meanwhile, yields rose an average of 4 bps for all maturities of 5 years and longer except for the 7-year maturity, which declined less than 1 bp. The uptick in longer tenors was driven by rising inflation, as consumer price inflation ticked up to 1.6% year-on-year (y-o-y) in January and December from 1.4% y-o-y in November but remained below the government's target range of 2.0%–3.5%.

## Local Currency Bond Market Size and Issuance

**Figure 2: Composition of Local Currency Bonds Outstanding in Malaysia**

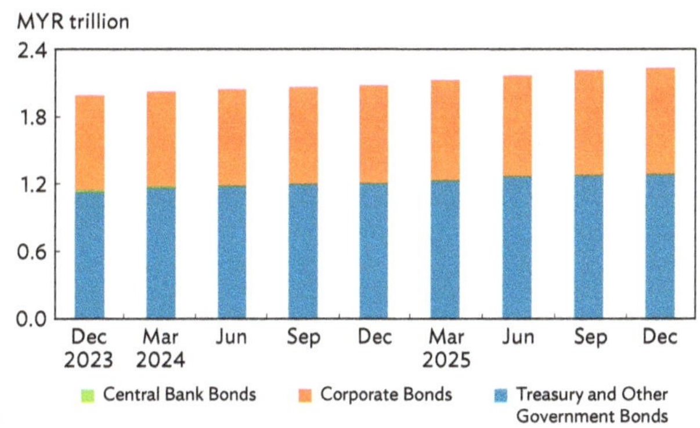


MYR = Malaysian ringgit.
Source: Bank Negara Malaysia Fully Automated System for Issuing/Tendering.

**Malaysia's local currency (LCY) bond market posted a slower expansion in Q4 2025, as issuance fell during the quarter.** Total LCY bonds outstanding increased 0.8% quarter-on-quarter (q-o-q) to MYR2.2 trillion, easing from the 2.2% q-o-q expansion recorded in the third quarter (Q3) of 2025 (**Figure 2**). Corporate bonds outstanding inched up 1.1% q-o-q in Q4 2025, decelerating from their 4.1% q-o-q gain in the prior quarter, as softer issuance and higher redemptions capped net growth. Meanwhile, the stock of Treasury and other government bonds advanced 0.5% q-o-q in Q4 2025, moderating from a 0.9% q-o-q expansion in the prior quarter, due to reduced issuance. *Sukuk* (Islamic bonds), remained the dominant segment of the LCY bond market, comprising 63.8% of total bonds outstanding at the end of December.

**Total LCY bond issuance contracted in Q4 2025, driven by reduced sales of government securities.** LCY bond issuance declined 14.5% q-o-q to MYR109.9 billion in Q4 2025, reversing the previous quarter's 48.1% q-o-q expansion (**Figure 3**). The issuance of Treasury and other government securities dropped 38.4% q-o-q as the Government of Malaysia had front-loaded annual borrowing earlier in the year. Corporate bond issuance edged up 4.0% q-o-q but moderated from the previous quarter's 55.0% growth due to a high base effect in Q3 2025 when companies took advantage of lower yields following a policy rate cut in July. State-owned PNB Merdeka Ventures accounted for the largest share (8.0%) of corporate issuance in Q4 2025 with issuance totaling MYR6.0 billion to finance property development projects.

This market summary was written by Justin Adrian Villas (consultant) in the Economic Research and Development Impact Department, Asian Development Bank, Manila.

**Figure 3: Composition of Local Currency Bond Issuance in Malaysia**

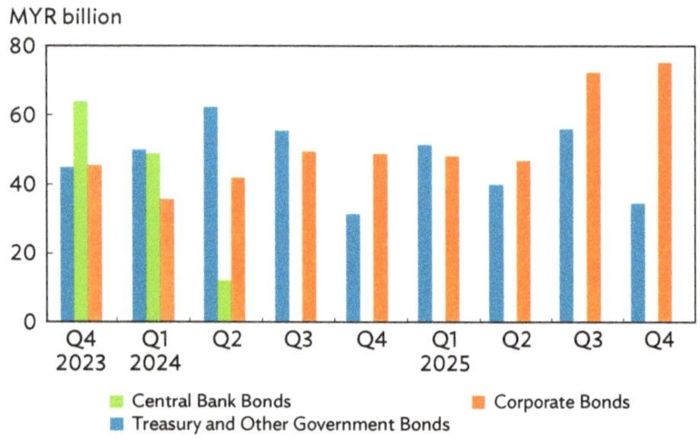


MYR = Malaysian ringgit, Q1 = first quarter, Q2 = second quarter, Q3 = third quarter, Q4 = fourth quarter.

Source: Bank Negara Malaysia Fully Automated System for Issuing/Tendering.

## Investor Profile

**At the end of September, domestic investors remained the largest investor group in Malaysia's LCY government bond market.** Collectively, domestic investors comprised 79.2% of total holdings in Malaysia's LCY bond market. Among these local investors, financial institutions and social security funds remained the largest investor groups, holding shares of 31.8% and 30.5%, respectively (**Figure 4**). Meanwhile, foreign holdings edged down to 20.8% from 22.4% a year earlier amid intermittent foreign outflows driven by weaker global risk sentiment and external trade-policy uncertainties. Malaysia nonetheless recorded one of the highest shares of foreign participation among emerging East Asian economies.[24]

**Figure 4: Local Currency Government Bonds Investor Profile**

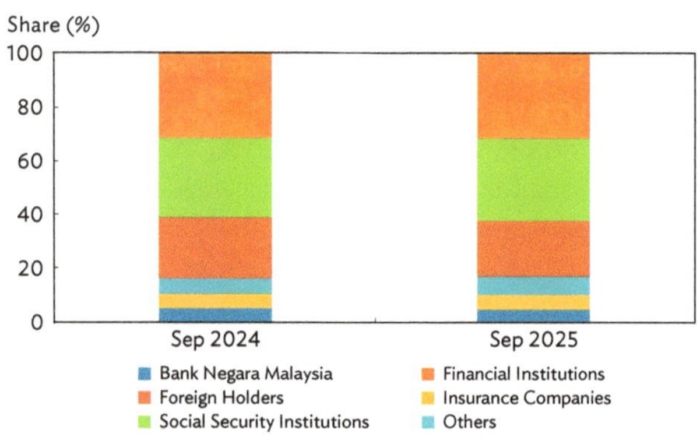


Note: "Others" include statutory bodies, nominees and trustee companies, and cooperatives and unclassified items.

Source: Bank Negara Malaysia.

## Sustainable Bond Market

**Malaysia's sustainable bond market continued to expand in 2025, buoyed by private sector issuance.** Outstanding sustainable bonds reached USD19.6 billion at the end of 2025, representing 2.6% of the emerging East Asian total (**Figure 5**). The market expanded 27.2% in 2025, accelerating from a 13.1% increase in 2024 amid increased private sector issuance. Private sector financing comprised 82.1% of total outstanding sustainable bonds and reached USD16.1 billion at the end of 2025. Private sector issuance climbed to USD4.9 billion on 67.3% y-o-y growth, supported by sales from PNB Merdeka Ventures, which issued USD1.4 billion worth of MYR-denominated sustainability *sukuk* as part of its funding diversification strategy. In contrast, the public sector has not issued any sustainable bonds since its last offering in 2023, but outstanding public sector sustainable bonds still comprised 17.9% of the total. At the end of 2025, 61.9% of outstanding sustainable bonds carried tenors exceeding 3 years, resulting in a size-weighted average tenor of 8.1 years. By instrument type, sustainability bonds accounted for 68.8% of the total, followed by green (18.1%), sustainability-linked (8.6%), and social (4.5%) bonds.

**Figure 5: Sustainable Bonds Outstanding in Malaysia**

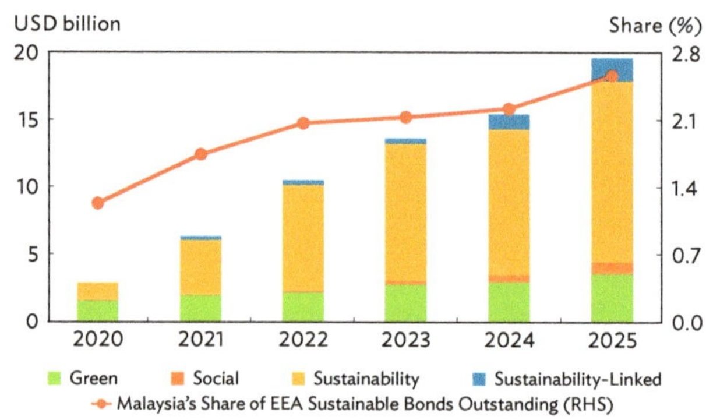


EEA = emerging East Asia, RHS = right-hand side, USD = United States dollar.

Notes:

1. Emerging East Asia is defined to include the member states of ASEAN plus the People's Republic of China; Hong Kong, China; and the Republic of Korea.
2. Data include both local currency and foreign currency sustainable bonds.
3. Sustainability-linked bonds include transition-linked bonds.

Source: *AsianBondsOnline* calculations based on Bloomberg LP data.

[24] Emerging East Asia is defined to include member states of the Association of Southeast Asian Nations plus the People's Republic of China; Hong Kong, China; and the Republic of Korea.

# Philippines

## Yield Movements

**Yields for short-term securities declined amid expectations of a February rate cut.** Between 3 November and 6 February, yields on local currency (LCY) government bonds with maturities of up to 7 years fell by an average of 23 basis points (bps) amid expectations that the Bangko Sentral ng Pilipinas (BSP) would cut its policy rate in February to support the economy (**Figure 1**). In the fourth quarter (Q4) of 2025, the Philippines' gross domestic product growth slowed to a 5-year low of 3.0% year-on-year (y-o-y) on weak household consumption and reduced government spending. As expected, the BSP reduced its policy rate by 25 bps on 19 February, following a rate cut in December. The BSP also noted that future policy direction depends on consumer confidence, which may recover in the coming months. The BSP's 5 February statement also noted that its rate-cutting cycle is nearing conclusion given benign inflation conditions, which pushed the yields for maturities of 10 years and longer to rise by an average of 12 bps during the review period.

**Figure 1: The Philippines' Benchmark Yield Curve—Local Currency Government Bonds**

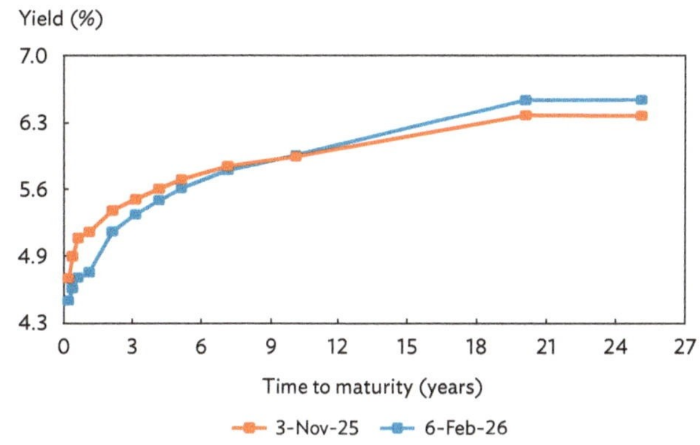


Source: Based on data from Bloomberg LP.

## Local Currency Bond Market Size and Issuance

**LCY bonds outstanding marginally declined in Q4 2025 due to a contraction in the stock of central bank securities.** Total LCY bonds outstanding edged down by 0.7% quarter-on-quarter (q-o-q) to PHP13.7 trillion at the end of December, extending the 0.1% q-o-q contraction in the previous quarter (**Figure 2**). The decline was mainly driven by a 43.6% q-o-q decline in the stock of central bank securities due to reduced issuance. Meanwhile, outstanding Treasury and other government bonds and corporate bonds recorded q-o-q gains of 1.2% and 2.1% in Q4 2025, respectively, as issuance volumes surpassed maturities.

**Figure 2: Composition of Local Currency Bonds Outstanding in the Philippines**

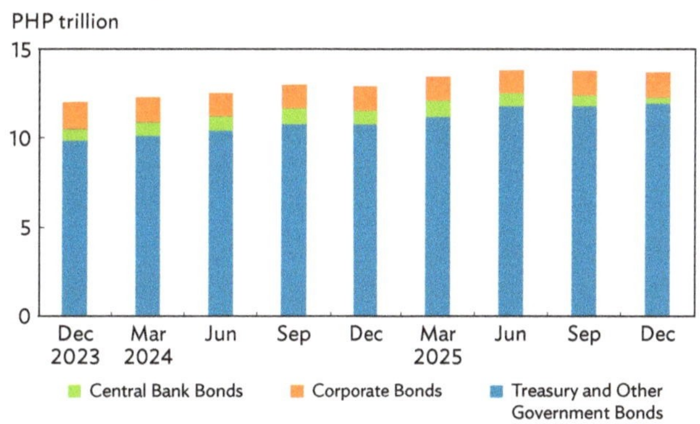


PHP = Philippine peso.

Note: Treasury and other government bonds comprise Treasury bonds, Treasury bills, and bonds issued by government agencies, entities, and corporations for which repayment is guaranteed by the Government of the Philippines.

Sources: Bangko Sentral ng Pilipinas, Bureau of the Treasury, and Bloomberg LP.

**Reduced bond sales were observed across all bond segments during the quarter.** Overall issuance tallied PHP1.7 trillion in Q4 2025, reflecting a 39.8% q-o-q drop from the previous quarter's PHP2.9 trillion (**Figure 3**). Issuance of Treasury and other government bonds posted contraction of 56.4% q-o-q as the government fulfilled most of its annual financing target in the preceding quarters. Similarly, corporate bond issuance fell 51.5% q-o-q in Q4 2025. Issuance of central bank securities declined 23.3% q-o-q as the BSP discontinued its 56-day securities since November.

This market summary was written by Jeremy Grace Ilustrisimo (consultant) in the Economic Research and Development Impact Department, Asian Development Bank, Manila.

**Figure 3: Composition of Local Currency Bond Issuance in the Philippines**

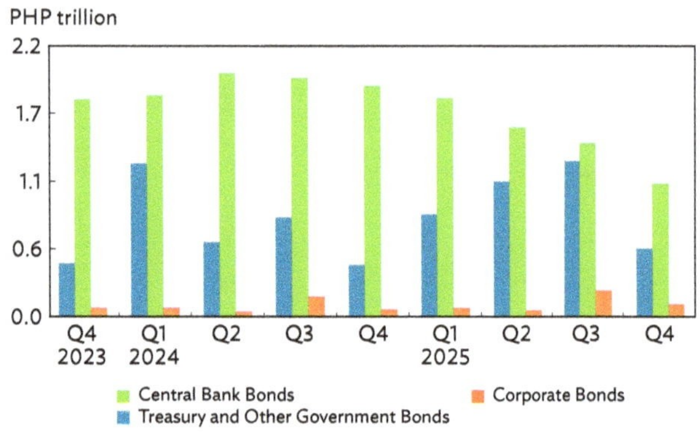


PHP = Philippine peso, Q1 = first quarter, Q2 = second quarter, Q3 = third quarter, Q4 = fourth quarter.

Note: Treasury and other government bonds comprise Treasury bonds, Treasury bills, and bonds issued by government agencies, entities, and corporations for which repayment is guaranteed by the Government of the Philippines.

Sources: Bangko Sentral ng Pilipinas, Bureau of the Treasury, and Bloomberg LP.

## Investor Profile

**The investor profile remained largely stable in 2025.** Banks and investment houses remained the largest investor group in the Philippines' LCY government bond market, with their share rising to 46.4% at the end of December from 45.3% a year earlier (**Figure 4**). Holdings by brokers, custodians, and depositories increased to 12.9% from 6.1% over the same period, while foreign holdings edged up to 4.8% from 4.2%, supported by improving market liquidity, transparency, and resilience, as well as optimism following JPMorgan's decision to place Philippine LCY government bonds on Index Watch-Positive in September 2025 for potential inclusion in its Government Bond Index for Emerging Markets. Market participants expect a final decision on the proposed 1% inclusion in March 2026. Meanwhile, the share held by contractual savings institutions and tax-exempt institutions stood at 21.2% in Q4, broadly similar to 21.5% in Q3. This was lower than 29.6% a year earlier and 28.1% in June 2025. The decline was largely driven by the BSP's reverse repo operations as part of its open market operations. These transactions materially affected the reported holdings under the tax-exempt institutions category and were a key factor behind the declines observed in Q3 and Q4 2025.

**Figure 4: Investor Profile of Local Currency Government Bonds**

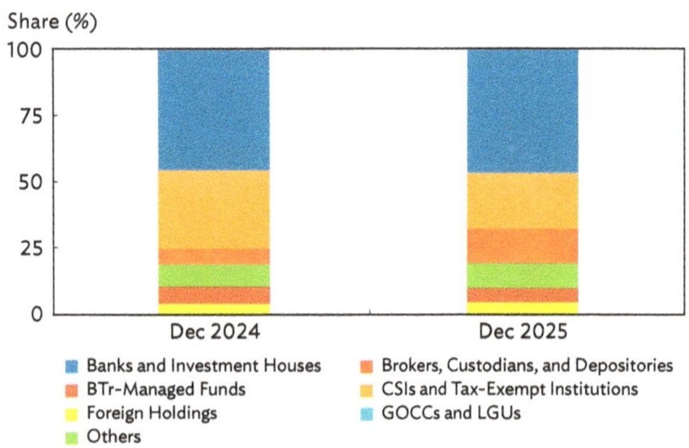


BTr = Bureau of the Treasury, CSI = contractual savings institution, GOCC = government-owned or -controlled corporation, LGU = local government unit.

Note: At the end of December 2025, the aggregate holdings share for GOCCs and LGUs was 0.001%, amounting to PHP0.2 billion.

Source: BTr.

## Sustainable Bond Market

**The Philippines' outstanding sustainable bonds totaled USD16.0 billion at the end of 2025.** The total sustainable bond stock increased 41.9% y-o-y in 2025, up from USD11.3 billion in 2024 (**Figure 5**). This lifted the Philippines' market share in emerging East Asia's total sustainable bond market to 2.1% from 1.6%.[25] The expansion was supported by strong investor demand, with total sustainable issuance tallying USD5.9 billion, about the same as the previous year's volume. Both the private (53.3%) and public (46.7%) sectors were active market participants, with over 90% of sustainable bonds from the public sector carrying tenors of more than 5 years.

**Figure 5: Sustainable Bonds Outstanding in the Philippines**

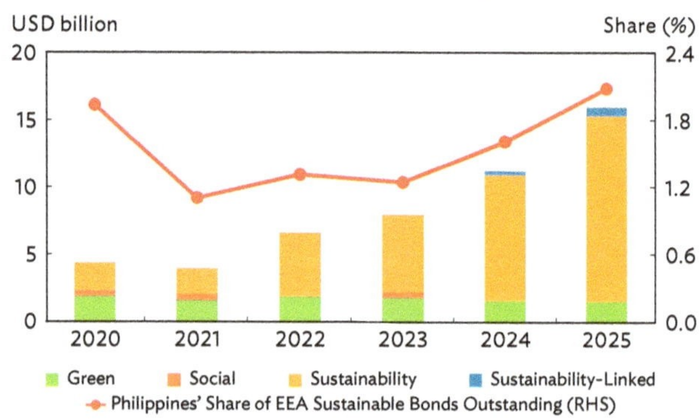


EEA = emerging East Asia, RHS = right-hand side, USD = United States dollar.

Notes:

1. Emerging East Asia is defined to include the member states of ASEAN plus the People's Republic of China; Hong Kong, China; and the Republic of Korea.
2. Data include both local currency and foreign currency sustainable bonds.
3. Sustainability-linked bonds include transition-linked bonds.

Source: *AsianBondsOnline* calculations based on Bloomberg LP data.

[25] Emerging East Asia is defined to include member states of the Association of Southeast Asian Nations plus the People's Republic of China; Hong Kong, China; and the Republic of Korea.

# Singapore

## Yield Movements

**Between 3 November and 6 February, local currency (LCY) government bond yields in Singapore largely tracked the yield movements of United States Treasuries.** Sovereign bond yields for maturities of 5 years and shorter (except 1-year bonds) ticked down an average of 3 basis points, while yields for maturities of 10 years and longer increased an average of 18 basis points (**Figure 1**). In addition to following the rise in yields for United States Treasuries, longer-dated LCY bond yields edged higher as domestic inflation trended upwards. On January, consumer price inflation rose to 1.4% year-on-year (y-o-y) from 1.2% y-o-y in December, driven by rising costs for accommodations and retail and other goods. In January, the Monetary Authority of Singapore (MAS) raised its inflation forecast for 2026 to 1.0%–2.0% from its October estimate of 0.5%–1.5%.

**Figure 1: Singapore's Benchmark Yield Curve—Local Currency Government Bonds**

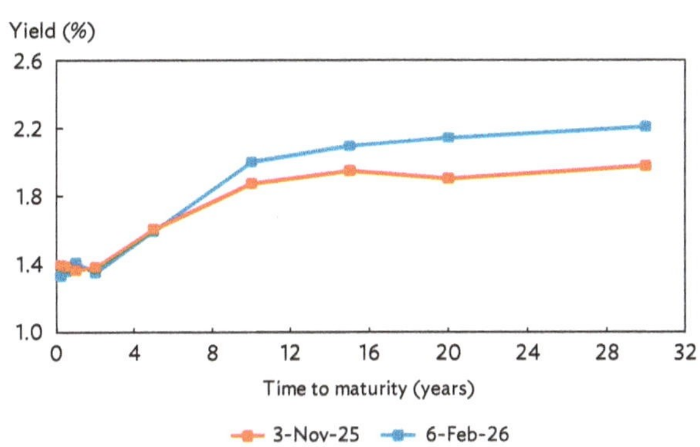


Source: Based on data from Bloomberg LP.

## Local Currency Bond Market Size and Issuance

**Singapore's LCY bond market was broadly unchanged in the fourth quarter (Q4) of 2025, totaling SGD896.9 billion.** During the quarter, modest corporate bond expansion was offset by slight contractions in government and central bank securities. Consequently, Singapore's total LCY bonds outstanding posted minimal growth of 0.03% quarter-on-quarter (q-o-q) in Q4 2025 (**Figure 2**). Outstanding corporate bonds inched up 0.7% q-o-q in Q4 2025 despite a contraction in issuance due to a lower volume of maturities during the quarter. Outstanding government securities and MAS bills narrowed 0.1% q-o-q and 0.3% q-o-q, respectively, partly due to reduced issuances during the quarter.

**Figure 2: Composition of Local Currency Bonds Outstanding in Singapore**

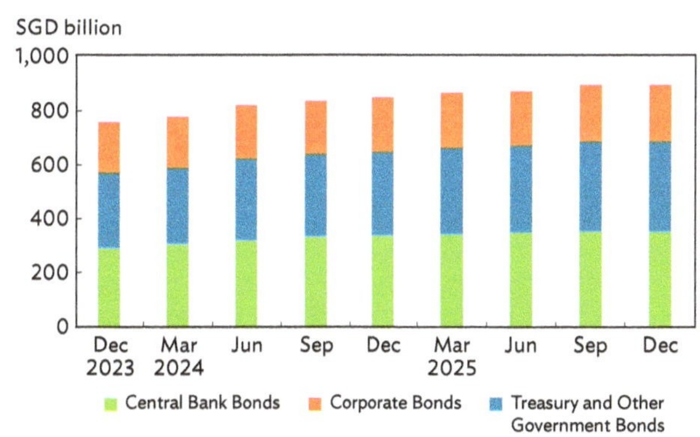


SGD = Singapore dollar.

Note: Corporate bonds are based on *AsianBondsOnline* estimates.

Sources: Monetary Authority of Singapore and Bloomberg LP.

This market summary was written by Justin Adrian Villas (consultant) in the Economic Research and Development Impact Department, Asian Development Bank, Manila.

**Total LCY bond issuance declined in Q4 2025 as bond sales weakened across all segments during the quarter.** Aggregate issuance contracted 2.6% q-o-q, falling to SGD556.8 billion, and extending the previous quarter's 0.3% q-o-q decrease (**Figure 3**). Total issuance was weighed down by reduced sales of MAS bills and Treasuries and other government securities, which decreased 1.6% q-o-q and 3.3% q-o-q, respectively. Corporate issuance fell 50.5% q-o-q primarily due to a high base effect. Issuance surged over sevenfold in the previous quarter, driven by a heavy volume of real estate bond sales. Almost half (45.7%) of corporate issuance in Q4 2025 came from the Housing and Development Board for the purpose of project funding.

**Figure 3: Composition of Local Currency Bond Issuance in Singapore**

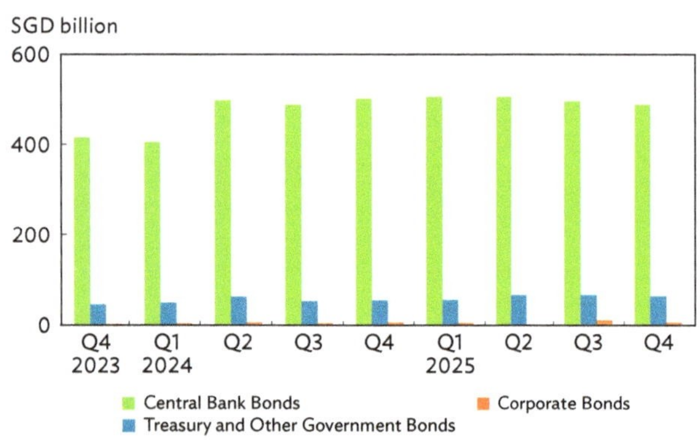


Q1 = first quarter, Q2 = second quarter, Q3 = third quarter, Q4 = fourth quarter, SGD = Singapore dollar.

Note: Corporate bonds are based on *AsianBondsOnline* estimates.

Sources: Monetary Authority of Singapore and Bloomberg LP.

## Sustainable Bond Market

**By end-2025, public and private sector issuers held comparable shares of Singapore's total outstanding sustainable bonds.** Singapore's sustainable bond market reached a size of USD32.6 billion at the end of 2025, accounting for 4.3% of the emerging East Asian total (**Figure 4**).[26] The sustainable bond stock expanded 25.6% y-o-y in 2025, extending the previous year's 43.4% y-o-y increase. Outstanding sustainable bonds from the private sector comprised 47.2% of the total at the end of 2025. Private sector issuance in 2025 amounted to USD3.1 billion, rising 29.7% y-o-y, led by bond sales from CapitaLand, which issued USD778.0 million worth of SGD-denominated green bonds for sustainability projects. Public sector bonds made up the remaining 52.8%, entirely consisting of green instruments. Public sector issuance tallied USD4.1 billion in 2025, including USD1.4 billion in SGD-denominated sovereign green bonds to serve as a benchmark to further develop Singapore's green finance market and to solidify its position as a regional sustainable finance hub. At the end of 2025, Singapore's size-weighted average tenor stood at 14.9 years, partly driven by outstanding sustainable bonds from the Government of Singapore, which carried tenors of 28 years and longer.

**Figure 4: Sustainable Bonds Outstanding in Singapore**

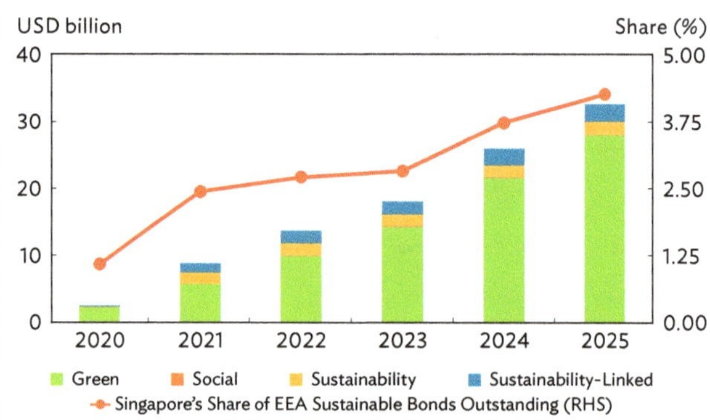


EEA = emerging East Asia, RHS = right-hand side, USD = United States dollar.

Notes:

1. Emerging East Asia is defined to include the member states of ASEAN plus the People's Republic of China; Hong Kong, China; and the Republic of Korea.
2. Data include both local currency and foreign currency sustainable bonds.
3. Sustainability-linked bonds include transition-linked bonds.

Source: *AsianBondsOnline* calculations based on Bloomberg LP data.

[26] Emerging East Asia is defined to include member states of the Association of Southeast Asian Nations plus the People's Republic of China; Hong Kong, China; and the Republic of Korea.

# Thailand

## Yield Movements

**Thailand's local currency (LCY) government bond yield curve steepened between 3 November and 6 February.** Yields fell an average of 12 basis points (bps) for bonds with maturities of up to 7 years but gained an average of 21 bps for bonds with longer maturities (**Figure 1**). Shorter-term bond yields declined as the Bank of Thailand resumed its policy easing cycle in December, after holding its rate steady during its 8 October meeting. To boost economic growth, the central bank reduced its policy rate by 25 bps to 1.25% at its 17 December meeting, and by another 25 bps to 1.00% during its 25 February meeting. Meanwhile, longer-term bond yields rose on expectations of increased government borrowing to fund the new administration's stimulus plans.

**Figure 1: Thailand's Benchmark Yield Curve—Local Currency Government Bonds**

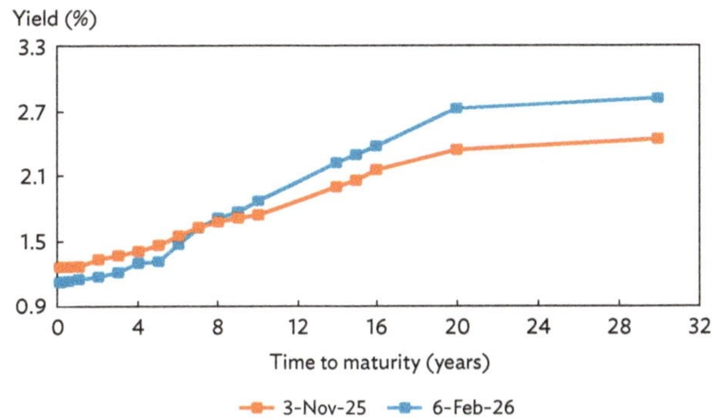


Sources: Based on data from Bloomberg LP and Thai Bond Market Association.

## Local Currency Bond Market Size and Issuance

**Thailand's LCY bond market edged up 1.1% quarter-on-quarter (q-o-q) in the fourth quarter (Q4) of 2025 to reach a size of THB17.8 trillion at the end of December.** The bond market's quarterly expansion slowed from the previous quarter's 2.5% q-o-q rise on a slower increase in government bonds and a contraction in corporate bonds (**Figure 2**). Government bonds outstanding reached THB10.7 trillion, with expansion moderating to 1.1% q-o-q in Q4 2025 from 2.0% q-o-q in the prior quarter due to reduced issuance and a larger volume of maturities. Meanwhile, corporate bonds outstanding (THB4.4 trillion) fell 0.1% q-o-q as the volume of maturities outpaced issuance.

**Figure 2: Composition of Local Currency Bonds Outstanding in Thailand**

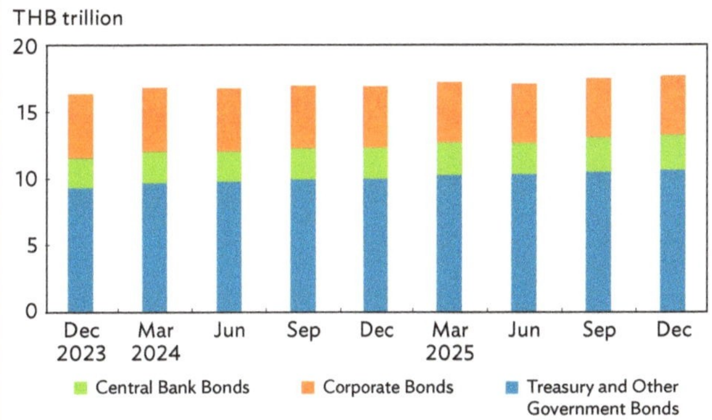


THB = Thai baht.
Sources: Bank of Thailand and Thai Bond Market Association.

**LCY bond issuance fell in Q4 2025 on reduced government borrowing and tepid corporate debt sales.** Issuance of new bonds edged down 0.9% q-o-q to THB2.2 trillion in Q4 2025, reversing the 2.6% q-o-q increase posted in the previous quarter (**Figure 3**). Government bond sales continued to contract, falling 5.3% q-o-q in Q4 2025 after a 16.5% q-o-q decline in Q3 2025. Government issuances in Q4 2025 included THB31.4 billion of sustainability-linked bonds (SLBs). Growth in corporate debt sales decelerated to 0.2% q-o-q in Q4 2025 from 8.7% q-o-q in the prior quarter as a surge in defaults dampened investor demand for new issues. Bond payment defaults rose to THB3.8 billion in Q4 2025 from THB2.2 billion in the previous quarter. Bond defaults were largely from capital-intensive companies that were heavily affected by the slowdown in domestic demand.

This market summary was written by Debbie Gundaya, consultant, Economic Research and Development Impact Department, Asian Development Bank, Manila.

**Figure 3: Composition of Local Currency Bond Issuance in Thailand**

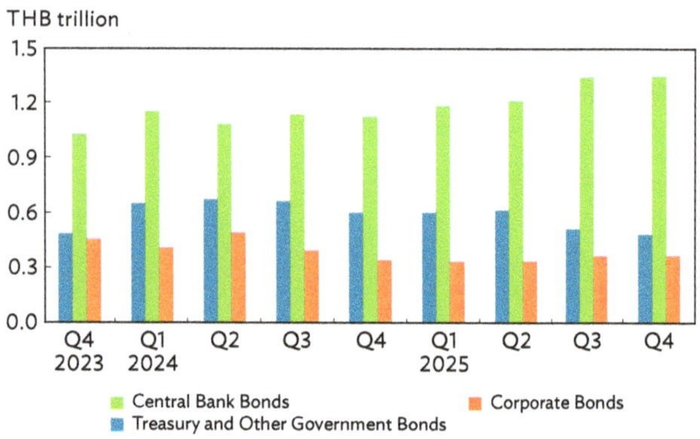


Q1 = first quarter, Q2 = second quarter, Q3 = third quarter, Q4 = fourth quarter, THB = Thai baht.

Sources: Bank of Thailand and Thai Bond Market Association.

**Figure 4: Investor Profile of Government Bonds in Thailand**

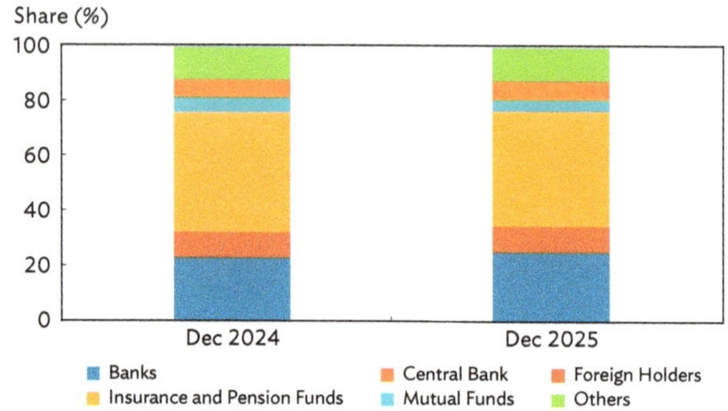


Source: Bank of Thailand.

# Investor Profile

**Banks and insurance and pension funds remained the primary holders of Thai Treasury bonds.** At the end of December, the holdings share of banks for Thai Treasury bonds increased to 25.5% from 23.3% a year earlier amid a contraction in loan growth. Meanwhile, the holdings share of insurance and pension funds inched down to 42.2% from 43.8%. These two investor groups remained the top holders of Thai Treasury bonds, with a combined holdings share of 67.6% at the end of December. The holdings share of other investor groups posted marginal changes. As such, the investor profile of Thai Treasury bonds was little changed in December from a year earlier (**Figure 4**).

**Figure 5: Sustainable Bonds Outstanding in Thailand**

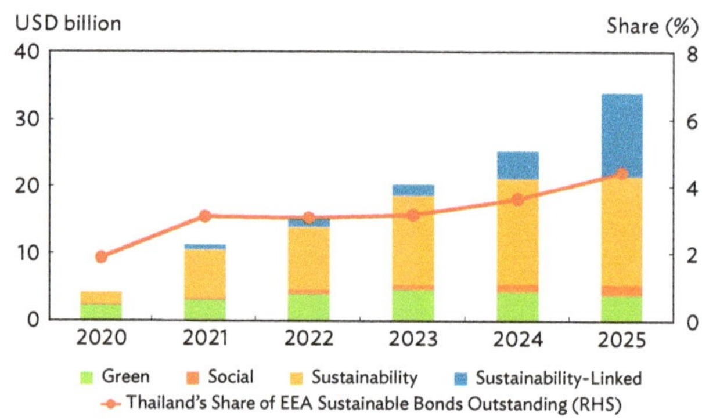


EEA = emerging East Asia, RHS = right-hand side, USD = United States dollar.

Notes:

1. Emerging East Asia is defined to include the member states of ASEAN plus the People's Republic of China; Hong Kong, China; and the Republic of Korea.
2. Data include both local currency and foreign currency sustainable bonds.
3. Sustainability-linked bonds include transition-linked bonds.

Source: *AsianBondsOnline* calculations based on Bloomberg LP data.

# Sustainable Bond Market

**The expansion of Thailand's sustainable bond market accelerated in 2025, propelled by robust issuance of SLBs.** The stock of sustainable bonds has steadily increased since 2020, reaching a size of USD34.0 billion at the end of 2025 (**Figure 5**). The market registered robust growth of 34.1% year-on-year in 2025, up from 24.6% year-on-year in 2024, driven largely by increased issuance of SLBs. While sustainability bonds remained the predominant type of sustainable bond instrument, comprising 47.5% of the total, the share of SLBs has increased markedly since 2024. In 2025, SLB issuance amounted to USD8.3 billion, representing 82.3% of total sustainable bond issuance. Almost 90% of SLB issuance in 2025 came from the public sector, largely from reopenings and bond switch transactions to an existing 15-year sovereign SLB.[27] The private sector also actively issued SLBs in 2025, with an equivalent of USD897.2 million of issuance.

[27] The 15-year government sustainability-linked bonds was launched on 25 November 2024 and was the first sovereign sustainability-linked instrument issued in Asia. At the end of December 2025, the bond had an outstanding amount of THB159.4 billion.

# Viet Nam

## Yield Movements

**Between 3 November and 6 February, local currency (LCY) government bond yields rose an average of 31 basis points across the curve (Figure 1).** The yield uptick was partly driven by an expected increase in the bond supply as the government plans to issue bonds worth VND500.0 trillion in 2026, 34.6% higher than the VND371.5 trillion worth of bonds issued in 2025. The expanded borrowing plan is intended to finance public investment projects, cover the budget deficit and debt repayments, and support attainment of the government's growth target of 10% for full-year 2026.

**Figure 1: Viet Nam's Benchmark Yield Curve—Local Currency Government Bonds**

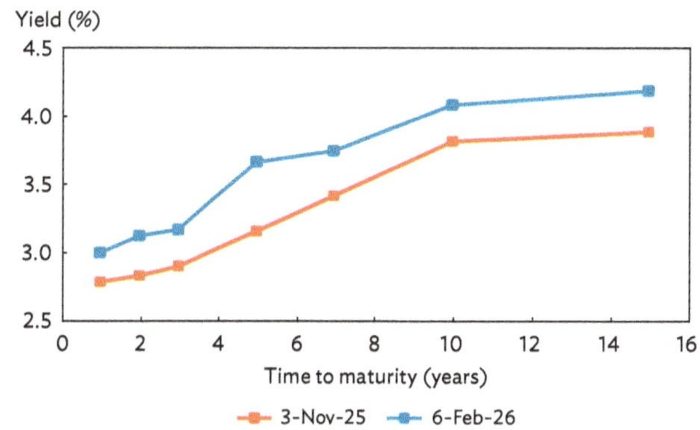


Source: Based on data from Bloomberg LP.

## Local Currency Bond Market Size and Issuance

**The LCY bond market's expansion accelerated in Q4 2025 on gains in both the government and corporate bond segments.** Outstanding LCY bonds reached VND3,972.9 trillion at the end of December, increasing 10.5% quarter-on-quarter (q-o-q) from VND3,595.8 trillion in the previous quarter (**Figure 2**). The government and corporate bond segments recorded accelerated q-o-q expansions of 4.5% and 7.0%, respectively, on increased issuance. Despite decreased q-o-q issuance in Q4 2025, central bank securities posted the fastest quarterly expansion among all bond types, reaching VND384.0 trillion of outstanding securities—more than double the previous quarter's VND185.0 trillion—due to a low volume of maturities during the quarter.

**Figure 2: Composition of Local Currency Bonds Outstanding in Viet Nam**

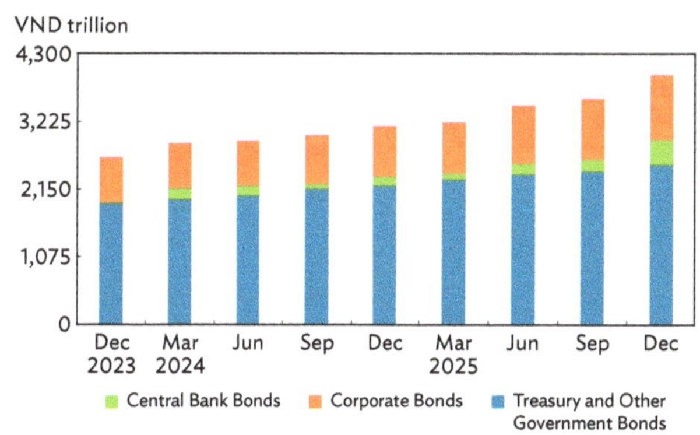


VND = Vietnamese dong.

Note: Other government bonds comprise government-guaranteed and municipal bonds.

Sources: Hanoi Stock Exchange, State Bank of Vietnam, Vietnam Bond Market Association, and Bloomberg LP.

**LCY bond issuance contracted in Q4 2025, driven by the reduced issuance of central bank securities.** In Q4 2025, LCY bond issuance tallied VND1,168.0 trillion, reflecting a 7.6% q-o-q drop from the previous quarter (**Figure 3**). The overall decline was mainly driven by the 17.1% q-o-q contraction in central bank securities issuance. Meanwhile, issuance of Treasury and other government bonds recorded the sharpest gain, more than twice the previous quarter's volume to VND121.9 trillion as the government ramped up bond sales to meet its full-year 2025 issuance target of VND500.0 trillion. At the end of 2025, the government completed about 74.3% (VND371.5 billion) of its bond issuance plan. Corporate bond issuance rebounded in Q4 2025, gaining 26.5% q-o-q after the previous quarter's 40.6% q-o-q contraction, as corporates accelerated their capital refinancing ahead of repayment pressure in December. The banking and property sectors remained the main drivers of issuance during the quarter, comprising 55.5% and 34.4%, respectively, of the market's Q4 2025 corporate issuance total.

This market summary was written by Jeremy Grace Ilustrisimo, consultant, Economic Research and Development Impact Department, Asian Development Bank, Manila.

**Figure 3: Composition of Local Currency Bond Issuance in Viet Nam**

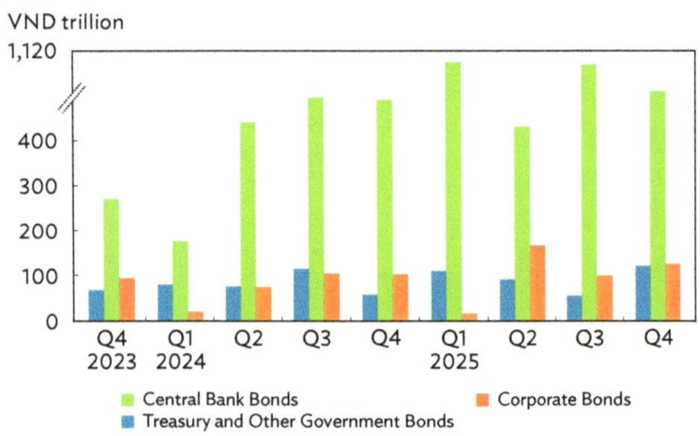


Q1 = first quarter, Q2 = second quarter, Q3 = third quarter, Q4 = fourth quarter, VND = Vietnamese dong.

Note: Other government bonds comprise government-guaranteed and municipal bonds.

Sources: Hanoi Stock Exchange, State Bank of Vietnam, Vietnam Bond Market Association, and Bloomberg LP.

## Investor Profile

**LCY government bonds outstanding remained largely held by two dominant investor groups.** Insurance companies, the largest investor group in Viet Nam's bond market, held 61.6% of the LCY government debt stock at the end of September, up from 59.8% a year earlier (**Figure 4**). In contrast, banks' investment share declined to 37.4% from 39.4% during the same period.

**Figure 4: Market Profile of the Two Dominant Investors for Local Currency Government Bonds**

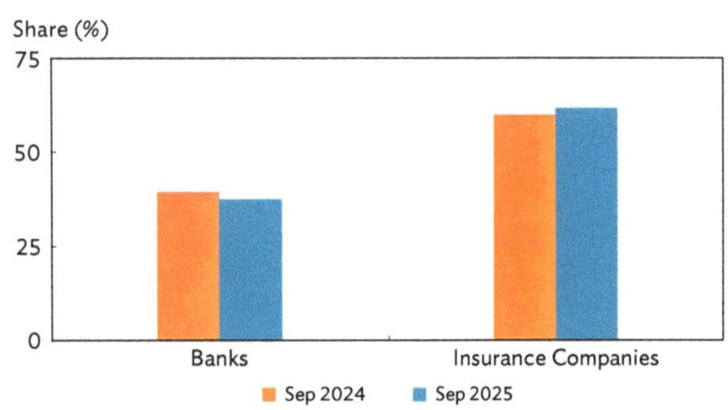


Source: Ministry of Finance, Viet Nam.

These two investor groups collectively accounted for 99.0% of the total LCY government debt stock at the end of September. This lack of investor diversity in the economy's bond market led to Viet Nam once again posting the highest Herfindahl–Hirschman Index score in the region.[28]

## Sustainable Bond Market

**Viet Nam's sustainable bond market was solely driven by the private sector.** Total sustainable bonds outstanding remained unchanged at the end of 2025 from a year earlier at USD1.1 billion, resulting in a slight dip (from 0.16% to 0.15%) in its share of emerging East Asia's sustainable bond market (**Figure 5**).[29] The economy's sustainable debt stock only comprises green and sustainability instruments, which accounted for 52.2% and 47.8%, respectively, of the 2025 sustainable bond market. About 80% of outstanding sustainable bonds carried tenors of 3 years or less, resulting in a size-weighted average tenor of 1.9 years, one of the shortest in the region. By currency profile, nearly 55% of outstanding sustainable bonds were denominated in United States dollars, while the remaining 45% were denominated in Vietnamese dong.

**Figure 5: Sustainable Bonds Outstanding in Viet Nam**

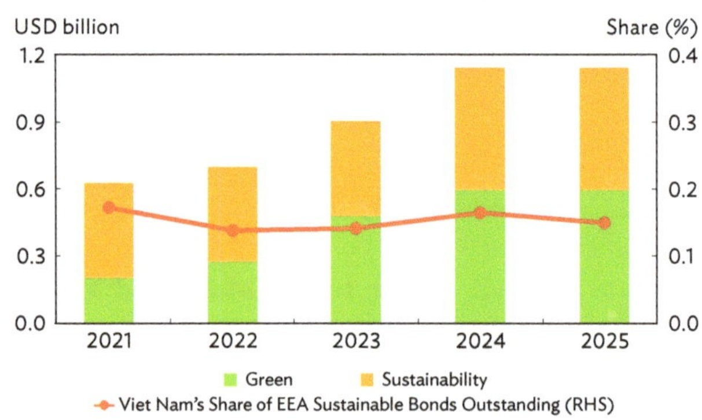


EEA = emerging East Asia, RHS = right-hand side, USD = United States dollar.

Notes:
1. Emerging East Asia is defined to include the member states of ASEAN plus the People's Republic of China; Hong Kong, China; and the Republic of Korea.
2. Data include both local currency and foreign currency sustainable bonds.

Source: *AsianBondsOnline* calculations based on Bloomberg LP data.

[28] The Herfindahl-Hirschman Index is a common measure of market concentration. The index is used to measure the investor profile diversification of the LCY bond market by summing the squared share of each investor group in the bond market.

[29] Emerging East Asia is defined to include member states of the Association of Southeast Asian Nations plus the People's Republic of China; Hong Kong, China; and the Republic of Korea.

www.ingramcontent.com/pod-product-compliance
Lightning Source LLC
Chambersburg PA
CBHW041800220926
51847CB00014B/273
*9789292777272*